INNOVATE OR STAGNATE

INNOVATE OR STAGNATE

The New Rules of Engineering Leadership

THOMAS HOLMENGREN

Imperial Book Publishing

Contents

Innovate or Stagnate

> *"The biggest room in the house*
> *is the room for improvement."*
> ~ Proverb

Preface

Welcome to *"Innovate or Stagnate: The New Rules of Engineering Leadership,"* a journey into the transformative world of software engineering. I'm Thomas Holmengren, and with over 25 years of experience spanning continents across Americas, Europe, Asia and Pacific, and navigating the diverse landscapes of industries from telecommunications to financial services, government projects, and currently working in the property and casualty insurance industry, I have seen it all.

My journey, which started with a passion for mathematics and coding and a Master's degree in Computer Science, has taken me from being a developer to leading global delivery teams, and now, to my role as a Senior Principal Software Engineer. I haven't just witnessed the evolution of this field; I've been right there in the thick of it, sometimes even getting my hands super dirty.

This book is born out of a deep-seated belief that software engineering is much more than just programming within the confines of a cubicle. Seriously, if you think it's just about churning out code, you're in for a surprise. It's a vibrant blend of art and science, requiring creativity, strategic thinking, and the ability to see beyond the immediate task to the broader impact of one's work. Yet, these critical facets are often overshadowed by conventional views that limit our appreciation of what engineers truly bring to the table. It's not just pizza and late-night caffeine indulges.

In "Innovate or Stagnate," we will delve into the creative heart of engineering, explore the nuanced skills that distinguish a good engineer from a great one, and challenge the critical misperceptions surrounding the value of skilled engineers in the corporate world. Each chapter is designed not just to inform but to inspire, inviting you to rethink how we value and invest in engineering talent. Trust me, you'll want to stick around for this.

Why this book? Because the future belongs to those who innovate. As technologies advance and industries evolve, the demand for engineers who are not only technically proficient but also able to lead and inspire continues to grow. Through my personal experiences (including a few hilarious missteps) and the lessons learned from colleagues around the world, I aim to illuminate the path for engineers and tech leaders alike, offering insights that bridge the gap between coding and leadership.

As we embark on this exploration together, I invite you to engage, question, and reflect. Whether you are an engineer, a tech leader, or simply curious about the field, there is something in these pages for you. Let's redefine what it means to be a software engineer in today's ever-changing world.

In these pages, you will discover strategies to foster innovation within your teams and learn how to cultivate an environment where top talent can thrive. You'll see how embracing creativity and allowing engineers the freedom to experiment leads to breakthroughs that can set your organization apart from the competition. It's not just about having a ping pong table in the break room.

We will also confront the pressing issue of artificial intelligence and its role in the future of software development. While some may view Artificial Intelligence (AI) with apprehension, fearing it will replace human jobs, this book will show how AI can be harnessed as a powerful tool to augment human creativity and efficiency. We'll discuss practical ways to integrate AI into your workflows securely and ethically, transforming it from a source of anxiety into an indispensable ally. Think of it as your friendly neighborhood Spider-Man, but for code.

Moreover, we will delve into the future roles and responsibilities that engineers must prepare for. As the landscape evolves, so too must the skills and approaches of those within it. The software engineer of tomorrow will need to be versatile, continually learning, and adept at both technical and soft skills. They will need to be architects of scalable systems, mentors to their peers, and strategic thinkers who understand the broader business implications of their work. Basically, you'll need to be the Swiss Army knife of engineers.

Finally, this book will draw a vivid parallel between the world of software engineering and the culinary arts. Just as anyone can cook but not everyone can be a chef, anyone can code, but not everyone can elevate their craft to the level of artistry required to innovate. By embracing the mindset of a chef where he or she is experimenting, refining, and striving for excellence so engineers can create solutions that are not just functional but transformative. So, grab your apron, because we're about to cook up some amazing ideas and strategies.

As you turn the pages of this book, I hope you find inspiration and practical guidance. I hope it challenges you to think differently about your role and the impact you can make. Let's embark on this journey together, embracing innovation and rejecting stagnation, to build a future where technology and creativity go hand in hand, driving us toward ever greater heights of achievement and satisfaction. And hey, if we can have a few laughs along the way, even better.

Chapter 1

The Creative Heart of Engineering

Welcome to the magical realm of software engineering, where creativity is often overshadowed by lines of code and technical jargon. But let's face it, without creativity, we'd all still be banging rocks together to start a fire. Creativity is the secret sauce that propels us forward, challenges the status quo, and births groundbreaking innovations. In this chapter, I want us to dive into the intrinsic role of creativity in software engineering, debunk the myth of the "code monkey," and showcase how leading engineers around the world harness creative thinking to solve complex problems.

First off, let me clear up a common misconception: Creativity in software engineering isn't about painting pretty pictures (though, if you can code and paint, more power to you!). It's about finding novel solutions to technical challenges, optimizing systems, and designing products that meet evolving user needs in unexpected and efficient ways. It's about thinking beyond the given parameters to reimagine what's possible. If you've ever had to creatively debug a piece of code at 2 o'clock in the morning with only caffeine and nothing else to guide you, you know what I'm talking about.

Creativity in software engineering transcends the mere aesthetic; it is a fundamental skill for solving complex problems, enhancing system functionality, and delivering user-centric solutions. It involves a deeper understanding of not only the technical requirements but also the end-user needs and the broader business objectives. This form of creativity is essential for developing products that are not only functional but also innovative and efficient in ways that significantly improve user experience.

In the territory of software engineering, creativity is characterized by the ability to break away from traditional methods and explore new possibilities. This might mean devising a different algorithm that optimizes performance beyond established benchmarks or developing a user interface that revolutionizes how users interact with the software. It's about leveraging technology in ways that were not thought possible, turning theoretical ideas into practical solutions that push technological boundaries.

At the heart of every groundbreaking software solution lies a creative spark. It is about seeing beyond the usual approaches and imagining what could be, not just what is. Consider, for example, the challenge of system integration faced by many organizations. Each system or application in a company's arsenal might serve its purpose well but imagine the inefficiency of building separate integration solutions for each one. It's like trying to invent a new wheel every time you need to get somewhere. Ridiculous, right? And yet, we do it all the time.

Many outside the tech world view coding as a straightforward, almost mechanical process. However, those of us who engineer software know it's as much about innovation and artistry as it is about technical proficiency. It involves seeing beyond the typical solutions, envisioning what could be achieved with a blend of creativity and technical acumen. Picture it like this: coding without creativity is like baking without sugar. Sure, you can do it, but no one's going to want to eat what you make.

Consider the scenario where an organization needs to integrate analytics, customer data, management systems, or any other systems for that matter. Do we take the conventional route? We develop multiple integration models, one for each pairing of systems. Or we create a more creative, efficient solution? We architect and develop a common integration framework that can be customized for each specific need, reducing redundancy, saving time, and decreasing the likelihood of errors. It's like creating a universal remote for all your devices instead of juggling a dozen different ones.

This isn't just a theoretical concept. In my experience, applying such a framework not only streamlined operations but also empowered the engineering team to think more strategically about problem-solving. We transformed a routine task into a creative challenge, finding a solution that was both elegant and practical. And let's be honest, who doesn't love a good challenge that also makes life easier? I know I do. Because in the world of software engineering, it's not just about writing code; it's about writing the future.

Creative thinking in software engineering is like the secret ingredient in your grandma's legendary spaghetti sauce. It's what takes something from good to unforgettable. How can we do it?

Problem Reframing: Imagine being handed a problem and being told, "Fix it!" That's like being asked to bake a cake without being given any sugar. I have been told that numerous of times. And that is when we, creative engineers, look at the problem from different angles to uncover the root causes and wider implications.

For instance, if you're dealing with slow data retrieval in a database, the typical response might be to optimize the queries. Usually, project managers will tell us to optimize the query. Some good engineers will also go that route. But what would a creative engineer do? They'd step back and ask, "What if the whole data architecture needs an overhaul?" This might lead to a more holistic solution, like implementing a distributed database system or using a caching mechanism to speed up data access. Think of it as deciding to bake cookies instead of a cake. They are still delicious, but way more efficient!

Innovative Problem Solving: This is where we throw convention out the window and start experimenting. Remember when fraud detection used to mean sifting through endless transaction logs manually? A creative engineer might think, "Why not let the machines do the heavy lifting?" They'd develop a machine learning algorithm that can spot suspicious activities faster than a cat catching a laser pointer. This not only reduces the need for human intervention but also makes the process way more accurate and efficient.

Optimizing Systems: Imagine a hospital where patient management systems, billing systems, and electronic health records (EHR) don't talk to each other. It's chaos, like trying to cook a five-course meal in a kitchen where the oven doesn't speak to the stove. Creative engineers create middleware or an integration framework that allows these systems to communicate seamlessly, reducing operational lag and improving data flow. It's like finally getting all your kitchen appliances to work together in harmony and suddenly, everything runs smoother, and dinner's on the table faster.

Design Thinking: Here's where we channel our inner Steve Jobs. Design thinking focuses on user-centric designs that prioritize usability and accessibility. Take a new mobile banking app, for instance. A creative engineer conducts user interviews and iterates prototypes, ensuring the final product is intuitive and accessible to users of all ages and tech skills. It's like designing a kitchen that even your tech-challenged grandma can use without calling you every five minutes. And we do not want to be called every five minutes. I will talk about interruptions and how annoying they are in the next chapters.

At its core, creativity in software engineering is about re-imagining what's possible. Engineers must envision future scenarios and anticipate needs that users themselves might not even be aware of yet. This forward-thinking approach often leads to the development of breakthrough technologies that set new industry standards and open up new markets.

For example, think about the evolution of smartphone touch interfaces. Before touchscreens, physical keyboards were the norm. I loved my Blackberry. Well until I switched to iPhone. The leap to touch interfaces required a deep understanding of user ergonomics, software integration, and material science. It's like going from riding a bicycle to driving a Mercedes. It is the exact same concept, but vastly different experience.

Or consider the development of a smart home system. Instead of creating isolated smart devices, a creative approach integrates them into a cohesive ecosystem controlled by a central hub with AI capabilities. It's like having a personal assistant who knows you so well that your coffee is ready when you wake up, the lights adjust to your mood, and the thermostat keeps things just right. Basically, a home that loves you back.

By embracing creative thinking, software engineers can move beyond the obvious and conventional, paving the way for groundbreaking innovations and more efficient, user-friendly solutions. Creativity in software engineering is not just about writing code; it's about envisioning new possibilities and bringing them to life in ways that significantly enhance functionality and user experience. So, let's roll up our sleeves, sprinkle in some creativity, and start cooking up some innovative solutions! Creativity does matter, and below I would like to discuss why.

Why Creativity Matters

Alright, let's get one thing straight: creativity in software engineering isn't just about making your code look like a Picasso painting. It's about reimagining processes, boosting efficiencies, and crafting solutions that are not only effective but revolutionary. Why does this matter? There are three main reasons why and those are efficiency, scalability and competitive edge.

Efficiency: Creative solutions do more than solve problems; they redefine the entire process of solving them. It's like realizing you don't need a spoon to eat soup. We can just drink it straight from the bowl. By thinking creatively, engineers can cut out unnecessary steps, integrate snazzier technologies, and optimize workflows. Imagine rethinking a data entry system to automate repetitive tasks. Suddenly, those precious hours spent on mind-numbing manual input are freed up for more important things, like debating whether to have pizza or tacos for lunch. Seriously, if I need to do the same task more than once, I will find any way possible to automate it. One reason is because I am lazy but also I do not want to do the same task again. But the result is efficiency.

Scalability: Innovative approaches are designed with the future in mind. It's like buying stretchy pants for Thanksgiving because we are definitely anticipating growth. Creative solutions are inherently more adaptable, making it easier for businesses to scale without tearing down their whole operation and starting from scratch. This foresight minimizes disruptions and the need for costly, frequent upgrades as user demands evolve or as the business expands. It's about building a system that grows with you, kind of like that pet iguana you swore wouldn't get too big.

Competitive Edge: In today's turbo-charged market, being first to the party can be a game-changer. Companies that foster a culture of creativity encourage their engineers to experiment and innovate. This often leads to breakthrough products and services that hit the market first, setting the company apart from competitors. It's like showing up to a potluck with a gourmet dish when everyone else brought chips. For instance, creative cloud solutions can enable a company to offer unique customer experiences that are secure, scalable, and efficient, and often before these features become industry standards. Basically, you're the trendsetter everyone else is scrambling to keep up with.

Creativity in software engineering isn't just some fluffy, feel-good concept. It's a fundamental necessity. It empowers engineers to think outside the box (or the cube, or the hexagon, or whatever shape we're working with now), pushing the boundaries of what's possible and setting new standards for efficiency, scalability, and innovation. A creative mindset allows engineers to foresee potential challenges and opportunities, ensuring that solutions are not just reactive but proactive. This positions businesses for long-term success, kind of like always keeping a stash of chocolate for those inevitable late-night coding sessions.

Creativity fosters an environment where innovation thrives. In the ever-changing world of technology, this is crucial. By encouraging creative thinking, organizations can cultivate a workforce that's not only adept at solving current problems but also capable of envisioning and constructing the future of technology. It's about having a team that can dream big, think differently, and laugh in the face of the routine.

In conclusion of why creativity matters, the essence of creativity in software engineering lies in its ability to transform the ordinary into the extraordinary. It's about seeing beyond the immediate problem to the broader possibilities, leveraging both technical skill and imaginative thinking to create solutions that are not only functional but transformative. As we move forward in the ever-evolving landscape of technology, let's remember that creativity is the key to unlocking the full potential of software engineering. It's what drives progress and helps us achieve excellence. So, next time you're stuck on a problem, channel your inner artist, and remember that sometimes, the best solutions come from the wildest ideas.

The Underestimated Role
of Engineers in Creativity

Many companies and organizations hire engineers and developers with a very narrow expectation and that is to just execute predefined tasks, much like a robot programmed to follow a script. But let's face it, treating engineers as mere code jockeys vastly underestimates their true potential. Engineers are not just executors; they are inventors and innovators. They possess a unique blend of technical skills and logical thinking necessary to devise creative solutions. They can see patterns, predict potential issues, and innovate within constraints. They possess skills that are critical in today's complex technological landscape. And these skills should not be underestimated.

When organizations fail to recognize the full potential of their engineers, they miss out on a treasure trove of untapped creativity and problem-solving prowess. Engineers are often seen through the lens of their technical abilities alone, but their capacity for innovative thinking is equally vital. These are the folks who, when given a problem, don't just solve it; they twist it, turn it, and sometimes flip it upside down to see it from every angle. This kind of thinking can lead to breakthroughs that leave traditional approaches in the dust.

Moreover, when companies acknowledge the creative contributions of engineers, they can leverage these skills to drive business strategy. Engineers who are encouraged to think creatively often identify new opportunities to leverage technology for business growth. Imagine developing new software tools that open up additional revenue streams or improving system efficiencies to cut costs significantly. By involving engineers in strategic discussions, organizations can benefit from their unique perspectives and innovative ideas, and who knows, they might even come up with the next big thing during a coffee break.

Additionally, if we truly empower engineers to be creative it can lead to higher job satisfaction and retention. And who doesn't want that. Picture this: an engineer given the freedom to experiment and innovate is like a kid in a candy store. They are more likely to feel valued and motivated, which in turn enhances their productivity and commitment to the company. This approach fosters a culture of continuous improvement and innovation, where new ideas are welcomed and nurtured. It's like turning your engineering team into a perpetual motion machine of creativity and productivity.

By understanding and harnessing the creativity of engineers, companies not only enhance their product offerings but also cultivate a workforce that is proactive, motivated, and deeply engaged with their work. This leads to better solutions and fosters a culture of continuous improvement and innovation. As we advance into an increasingly digital future, the companies that will thrive are those that recognize the strategic importance of creativity and are adept at nurturing this talent within their ranks.

Organizations must shift their perspective and acknowledge that engineers are not just problem solvers. The companies and organizations must acknowledge that we are creators. This mindset change is crucial for fostering an environment where innovation can flourish. Encouraging engineers to explore, experiment, and take risks can lead to breakthroughs that drive the company forward in ways that rigid, task-oriented approaches cannot. It's about creating a sandbox where they can build castles, not just follow blueprints.

Lets recognize that engineers are not just task executors; they are innovators and drivers of strategic growth. By expanding our expectations and recognizing their creative potential, we can achieve significant advancements and maintain a competitive edge in the fast-paced tech world. Let's stop viewing engineers as mere code-writers and start appreciating them as the creative powerhouses they are.

Check out the visual below. It highlights just how powerful a creative environment can be for our engineering teams. When we prioritize creativity over rigid instructions, we give engineers the freedom to blend their technical know-how with innovative thinking. This not only boosts efficiency but also sparks fresh ideas. By fostering this culture of creativity, we pave the way for company growth through new products and improved processes. Let's unleash the full potential of our teams!

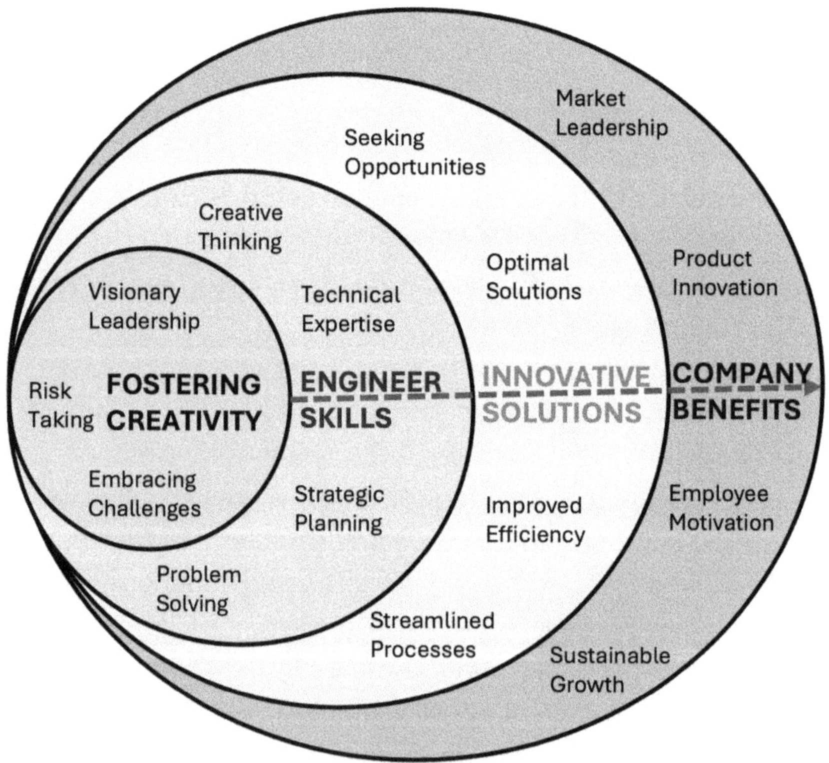

From Creativity to Growth
Thomas Holmengren

Conclusion: The Best Way Forward

So, how do we determine the 'best' solution? It starts with fostering a culture where engineers are encouraged to think like artists. Yes, you heard me, artists! We are artists, chefs. We need our engineers to feel free to experiment, innovate, and not just find any solution, but the optimal one. In a field as dynamic as software engineering, being technically adept isn't enough, and I will talk more about that in one of the next chapters. Our creativity is the engine of progress, distinguishing us within the tech industry and beyond. And let's face it, who wants to be just another cog in the machine when you can be the engine driving it forward?

Creativity in software engineering is not an optional extra; it's a necessity for staying relevant and competitive in this rapidly evolving technological landscape. By embracing a creative mindset, engineers can lead the charge in innovation, crafting solutions that are not only technologically advanced but also deeply integrated with the needs of the users and the strategic goals of their organizations. It's about thinking big, taking risks, and sometimes, just sometimes, breaking a few rules to make something truly extraordinary.

Moreover, creating a trust-based culture is essential for innovation to flourish. Imagine a world where engineers work in an environment free from fear, no fear of failure, no fear of stepping outside the norm, and certainly no fear of dissent. Sounds like a utopia, right? Well, it's achievable. I know it is. Trust is the foundation that allows creativity to thrive. Managers and leaders must trust in the creative processes and provide the tools and space necessary for such creativity to blossom. It's about giving your team the freedom to explore, to fail, and to learn. Because let's be honest, some of the best ideas come from the most unexpected failures.

This approach isn't just for individual projects or products; it forms the basis of a sustainable business strategy. Companies that invest in nurturing the creative talents of their engineers and instilling a culture of trust and support are better positioned to lead and succeed in the global marketplace. These companies aren't just developers of technology; they are pioneers of innovation, capable of profoundly impacting the world. They're the ones who turn 'what if' into 'what now,' and 'can we' into 'we did.'

Let us, therefore, embrace this shift towards a more innovative and trust-filled engineering culture. It starts with you. Encourage your teams to think big, to break molds, and to build not just what is easy, but what is extraordinary. This is how we redefine the essence of engineering. This is how we create futures that once seemed beyond our reach. So, let's expand our understanding, challenge the norms, and together prove that in the realm of software engineering, creativity is indeed our greatest asset. And who knows, maybe one day we'll look back and say, "Remember when we used to play it safe? What were we thinking?"

Chapter 2

The Hidden Cost of "Just a Quick Question"

PROTECTING THE FLOW OF ENGINEERING CREATIVITY

Now that we've established that creativity and thinking outside the box are essential, let's dive into how our creativity gets shattered by interruptions. Every time someone says, "I have a quick question," I roll my eyes so hard they do a full somersault. It's like I'm in the middle of perfectly searing a steak, and someone interrupts with, "Oh, quick question: can you explain the theory of relativity?" Well, thanks, now my steak is burnt, and the question might be quick, but the answer definitely is not. Plus, you just destroyed my cognitive flow. Let me explain it to you what I mean.

In today's high-speed, interconnected work environments, interruptions are often seen as minor inconveniences. However, for engineers who thrive on deep focus and creative flow, even a seemingly harmless "just a quick question" can be disproportionately disruptive. This chapter explores the profound impact of such interruptions on engineering productivity and the hidden costs they impose on organizations.

There are several researches performed and they indicate that it takes an average of about 20 to 30 minutes for an individual to fully regain their focus after an interruption. So, when we are pulled away from complex tasks, the disruption extends beyond just the lost minutes. It affects our ability to maintain a mental map of the project, disrupts our creative process, and can lead to errors or subpar work quality.

Interruptions not only delay the task at hand but also degrade the quality of work. Engineers are often in the midst of formulating solutions or debugging intricate code when interrupted. The break in concentration required to address even simple queries can reset their thought process, which then requires significant mental energy and time to restore.

Interruptions are more than just minor annoyances in the world of software engineering; they are significant disruptors of cognitive flow. When engineers engage in high-concentration tasks such as debugging intricate code or architecting complex systems, their brains operate at peak cognitive efficiency. These tasks require maintaining a highly detailed and sophisticated mental map of the project at hand. Interruptions, even those that seem minor, can have disproportionately large effects on the progress and quality of work. We need to understand this cognitive flow in engineering tasks.

Have you ever found yourself so engrossed in a task that you lose track of time? That's cognitive flow, a state every engineer strives to achieve. For me, it usually happens late at night with a cup of tea by my side, when world is quiet, when my dog is sleeping, and I can fully immerse myself in the code. But achieving this flow is like balancing on a tightrope. The flow is very fragile and easily disrupted.

Cognitive flow in software engineering is a state where an engineer is fully immersed in a task, with a heightened focus that enhances creativity and productivity. Achieving this state can take time and, once reached, is fragile and easily disrupted. This flow state is crucial for deep work. This is where complex problem-solving and innovative thinking occur.

I remember one particular instance where I was deep into debugging a complex algorithm, that I wrote. The algorithm was so complex I couldn't believe I came up with it at some point in time. Suddenly, "a quick question" from a colleague pushed me out of my focus. That simple interruption cost me nearly an hour to get back on track. It is moments like these that highlight the true cost of disruptions and the importance of protecting our cognitive flow. Now imagine few of those throughout the day.

In this chapter I will share strategies on how to minimize interruptions and maintain your mental map, ensuring you can work at your peak creativity and productivity. We must safeguard our most valuable asset: our focus. But before we do that lets talk more about cognitive flow, as we truly must understand what it is, so we know what we are protecting.

Formulating Solutions: When engineers are devising solutions, they are often considering multiple variables and potential outcomes simultaneously. This kind of multitasking is highly sensitive to disruption. An interruption forces the brain to switch contexts, which can obliterate the delicate structure of thought that was supporting the problem-solving process. For example, if an engineer is developing a new algorithm, they might be balancing efficiency, scalability, and ease of implementation in their mind. A sudden interruption can cause them to lose track of these considerations, forcing them to rebuild their mental model from scratch when they return to the task.

Debugging Intricate Code: Debugging is particularly susceptible to the detrimental effects of interruptions. It involves tracing paths through code, predicting where issues might arise, and keeping multiple potential fixes in mind. Interruptions can cause engineers to lose their place in the code or forget the reasoning behind a chosen debugging path, leading to time-consuming and costly mistakes. For instance, if an engineer is debugging a complex issue that requires understanding the interactions between several modules, an interruption can cause them to lose the context and the intricate understanding of the code flow they had built up. This can lead to a significant loss of productivity as they need to re-establish this context upon returning to the task.

Maintaining cognitive flow is thus essential for high-quality software engineering. Organizations can support this by creating an environment that minimizes interruptions and fosters deep work. This might include strategies such as designated quiet times, using collaboration tools that reduce the need for face-to-face interruptions, and encouraging a culture that respects focused work periods, and we will expand on that later in this chapter.

Understanding and protecting cognitive flow can lead to higher productivity, fewer errors, and more innovative solutions, ultimately benefiting both engineers and the organizations they work for. By acknowledging the importance of uninterrupted work time, companies can help engineers stay in their cognitive flow, maximizing their creativity and effectiveness.

So next time you think about asking "just a quick question," consider the potential cost of that quick interruption. It might just be worth waiting until the engineer has finished cooking their cognitive steak. After all, nobody likes a burnt steak or a half-baked solution.

Why 'Just a Quick Question' Is More Expensive Than It Seems

Every time my focus is shattered by an interruption, it feels like I'm trying to piece together a puzzle with the lights turned off. Getting back into that flow state isn't just about remembering where I left off; it's about re-engaging the intricate web of thoughts that were driving my creativity and problem-solving. The cost of these interruptions is steep, impacting both productivity and the quality of our work.

Each interruption might seem minor, but cumulatively, they represent a significant drain on productivity and innovation. The phrase "just a quick question" is often used in workplaces, but for engineers engaged in complex, creative problem-solving, these interruptions are anything but quick. Each pause to answer a query forces an engineer out of their cognitive flow, leading to a cascade of detrimental effects.

Time Cost: Rebuilding the mental map after an interruption is no small feat. Research shows that it can take about 20 to 30 minutes on average to get back to where I was before someone broke my concentration. Imagine if I get interrupted five times a day. Well, that's potentially 150 minutes lost just to regain focus, not to mention the actual interruptions themselves. This lost time adds up, turning a productive day into a scramble to catch up. It's like trying to finish a marathon when someone keeps moving the finish line further away.

Quality Degradation: When I finally return to my task, the quality of my work often takes a hit. The solutions I come up with might not be as thorough or innovative as they could have been if my flow had remained uninterrupted. This can result in software that's less efficient, less creative, and riddled with more bugs. For example, if I'm optimizing an algorithm and get interrupted, I might lose track of the fine-tuned improvements I was working on. When I get back to it, I might just settle for a quick fix to regain momentum, sacrificing the overall quality of the project.

Frequent interruptions don't just steal my time; they ramp up stress and frustration. This stress can push me to rush through tasks, leading to mistakes that wouldn't have happened in a more focused state. These errors not only affect the task at hand but can create ripple effects, requiring even more time later to fix them.

Understanding these costs underscores the importance of protecting our cognitive flow. By minimizing interruptions and creating an environment that fosters deep work, we can significantly boost both productivity and the quality of the software we create. This approach doesn't just benefit us as individual engineers; it contributes to the overall success and innovation capacity of our entire organization. Let's respect the flow, keep interruptions to a minimum, and together, we can build something truly extraordinary.

We have already established that each interruption forces engineers to switch contexts, which can significantly burden cognitive resources. And this cognitive load of reorienting oneself to a complex task is substantial and can erode the overall efficiency of the engineer's workday.

Let's look at another real-life example. A software developer at my team was working on a critical algorithm improvement when frequently interrupted with questions about unrelated minor bugs. These interruptions actually led to a 40% drop in his coding efficiency, as measured over a two-week period. Each interruption forced him to mentally switch gears, leading to lost time not only during the interruptions but also in the time it took to regain his focus and reconstruct the mental map of the problem he was working on.

The hidden costs of these "quick questions" are not limited to the immediate disruption they cause. They also have broader implications for the quality and innovation of the work produced as we have discussed previously. Now we know the quality of work often suffers post-interruption. Engineers might resort to less optimal solutions because their train of thought was disrupted. For instance, a complex bug fix might end up being a patch rather than a robust solution, leading to future problems and inefficiencies.

When engineers are constantly interrupted, their ability to think creatively and innovate is significantly hampered. Creativity requires deep, uninterrupted thought. By constantly breaking this flow, we limit the potential for groundbreaking ideas and innovative solutions. Engineers need the mental space to experiment, fail, and iterate, which is essential for true innovation.

Another very important aspect of frequent interruptions can more likely lead to increased stress and decreased job satisfaction. Engineers might feel that their work environment does not respect their need for focused work time, leading to frustration and burnout. This can result in higher turnover rates, further affecting the productivity and morale of the team.

Every time an engineer's workflow is interrupted, not only is the current task delayed, but the ripple effects can push entire project timelines back. This is particularly true in software development, where tasks are often interdependent. Projects with frequent interruptions generally experience a 20-30% increase in their completion time, compared to similar projects with protected work time. Interruptions can be the enemy of accuracy. When I return to a task after an interruption, my brain needs time to rebuild the mental model it was operating with before the break. This reconstruction phase is ripe for errors and oversights.

Let me share a real-world example. At a high-profile software company I once worked with, we had a critical bug introduced into the code during a phase of frequent interruptions. This bug was traced back to a logic error made right after an engineer was interrupted. The cost of fixing this error post-launch? Five times higher than it would have been if we had caught it during the initial development phase. Talk about an expensive "quick question."

Understanding the true cost of these interruptions is crucial for fostering a productive and innovative work environment. By minimizing interruptions and creating a culture that respects focused work time, we can significantly enhance both the efficiency and creativity of our engineering teams. This approach doesn't just benefit us individually; it contributes to the overall success and innovation capacity of the company.

Strategies for Minimizing Interruptions

Given the high cost of interruptions on the productivity and creativity of software engineers, it is crucial for both organizations and individual engineers to adopt strategies that protect the deep work necessary for effective software development. These strategies should aim to minimize disruption and foster an environment conducive to sustained, focused work.

For Organizations:

- **Structured Communication Times:** Implement designated "open hours" during which engineers are available for discussions and meetings. This allows engineers to focus without interruption during other times, maintaining a deep state of concentration essential for complex problem-solving tasks.
- **Asynchronous Communication Tools:** Encourage the use of communication tools that allow questions and messages to be logged and addressed at a time that suits the engineer's workflow. Tools like Slack, JIRA, or Asana can be used to manage queries without demanding immediate attention, thus reducing the disruptive impact of real-time interruptions.
- **Education on Interruption Impact:** Conduct regular training sessions and distribute communications that educate all staff about the costs associated with interruptions. This helps cultivate a culture of respect and understanding for focused work periods, encouraging more mindful communication practices.

- **Physical and Digital Workspace Optimization:** Design workspaces; both physical and digital, that minimize noise and distractions. This might include setting up quieter zones, providing noise-canceling headphones, and using software that limits notifications during focus times.
- **Policy on Minimizing Interruptions:** Develop and implement a clear organizational policy that outlines how and when interruptions are permissible. Ensure this policy supports structured communication and respects individuals' need for uninterrupted work periods.

For Engineers:

- **Setting Clear Boundaries:** Engineers should communicate their preferred work times and boundaries to their colleagues. Making these preferences known can help reduce interruptions by aligning colleagues' expectations with the engineers' work schedules. Block off some time on your calendar, and make sure no meetings on Fridays.
- **Using 'Do Not Disturb' Modes:** Make use of 'Do Not Disturb' features on phones and communication platforms to signal to others that you are in a focus session. This simple tool can effectively manage others' expectations for immediate responses.
- **Time Management Techniques:** Adopt time management methods like the Pomodoro Technique, which involves intense focus periods followed by short breaks. This technique not only helps in managing distractions but also keeps the mind fresh and more resilient against interruptions.
- **Empowerment to Enforce Boundaries:** Engineers should be empowered by their managers and team leads to enforce their communicated boundaries without fear of repercussions. This empowerment helps in maintaining a

healthy work environment where deep work is protected and valued.

· **Regular Review and Adaptation of Strategies:** Continuously review the effectiveness of implemented strategies and remain open to adapting them based on what works best for individual preferences and the evolving dynamics of the team.

Conclusion: Fostering a Culture of Respect and Trust for Deep Work

Protecting the creative flow of engineers is not merely about minimizing interruptions but about fostering a culture that deeply respects and facilitates focused, deep work. This involves instituting thoughtful policies and supporting engineers in managing their workflows, enabling them not only to maintain productivity but also to enhance satisfaction and drive innovation within their teams.

Trust is the cornerstone of this culture. We will cover that in depth in the upcoming chapters. Yes, trust deserves an entire chapter for itself. The old notion that productivity is solely the result of continuous oversight is outdated and counterproductive, especially in creative and technical fields. True innovation often comes when the mind is allowed to explore ideas without constraints, sometimes in moments as informal as during a shower or a walk. Trusting engineers to manage their time and output effectively is crucial. It means understanding that the best ideas and solutions often come from uninterrupted thought processes, which can occur inside or outside traditional work environments.

Managers and team leaders play a pivotal role in this by not only minimizing unnecessary interruptions but also by demonstrating trust in their engineers' professional conduct and creative process. This trust should be evident in the way leaders communicate expectations and evaluate performance; focusing on outcomes and innovations rather than mere visibility and time spent at a desk.

Cultivating a company culture that understands and respects the cost of interruptions is crucial. This can be achieved through targeted education campaigns and clear policies on managing and minimizing interruptions. By understanding and addressing the real cost of "just a quick question," companies can make significant strides in protecting their engineers' productivity, improving project outcomes, and reducing costly errors.

Embracing this deeper awareness helps in fostering a more disciplined and respectful approach to workplace communication, particularly in environments where deep thinking and concentration are essential for success. When engineers are trusted and given the autonomy to work undisturbed, they are not only more likely to innovate but also more inclined to be engaged and motivated in their roles. As the proverb goes "When you trust a craftsman with his tools, he builds wonders; trust your engineers with their tasks, and they will create innovation."

As we move forward, let us recognize that fostering a culture of respect for deep work, underpinned by trust, is not just beneficial but essential for any organization aiming to lead and succeed in the competitive landscape of technology and engineering.

This deeper awareness helps in fostering a more disciplined and respectful approach to workplace communication, particularly in environments where deep thinking and concentration are essential for success.

Chapter 3

Rethinking Meetings: How Short, Frequent Sessions Hinder Productivity

So, we've tackled the beast of interruptions and why they're the arch-nemesis of our cognitive flow. Now let's talk about their equally annoying cousin: meetings. You know, those short, frequent sessions that seem harmless but are productivity's version of death by a thousand cuts. Imagine you're finally getting into the groove of solving that complex coding problem, and then; ding! It's time for another "quick" meeting. Ugh, right?

In the modern workplace, meetings are like a double-edged sword. They're essential for collaboration and decision-making, but man, can they be massive time-suckers if not handled right. This chapter dives into the dark side of traditional meeting structures, especially those pesky short, frequent sessions that break our concentration and drain our energy.

There's this widespread belief that shorter meetings are the epitome of efficiency. They're scheduled back-to-back with the noble intent of minimizing disruption. "I know you're busy, so I've only scheduled a short meeting," says the organizer, with the best intentions. But here's the kicker: this well-meaning approach is a productivity killer.

Let's get real, short meetings are often a mirage of efficiency. Why? Because we humans are inherently selfish when scheduling them. We think about ticking off our task list without considering the havoc we wreak on our colleagues' focus. It's like saying, "Hey, I've interrupted your deep work, but it's okay because it's quick!" Meanwhile, we're left trying to piece together our fragmented thoughts like a shattered mirror.

These brief pow-wows rarely wrap up with decisive outcomes. Instead, they breed a monster of follow-up meetings. So much for saving time! It's like fixing a leaky pipe with a band-aid; the problem persists, and before you know it, you're drowning in an endless loop of meetings that steal more time than they save.

It's time we shake things up and rethink our meeting habits. Meeting efficiency isn't about cramming as many short sessions into a day as possible. It's about effectiveness. Longer, well-planned meetings can actually save time and boost productivity. Shocker, right?

Picture a meeting that's given ample time for in-depth discussion, thoughtful decision-making, and minimal follow-ups. It respects your workflow, giving you those precious uninterrupted periods to dive deep into your work. This is especially crucial for us tech folks, where complex problem-solving is the name of the game.

Alright, let's dive into the mental gymnastics we all perform daily but rarely discuss: task switching and its cognitive toll.

Imagine gearing up for a marathon and then, right before the start, someone asks you to join a pie-eating contest. That's what it feels like for an engineer when they're deep in code and suddenly pulled into a meeting. Our brains need to warm up for the task at hand, activating the right neural networks and shutting out the irrelevant noise. When we're yanked away, it's like hitting the brakes on a speeding car, and it is not exactly smooth sailing. It takes mental preparation for tasks that must be allotted and allowed.

Do you ever feel like your brain just ran a marathon after switching tasks? Well, I know I do, and that's because of the dreaded "task switch penalty." Cognitive scientists say this penalty can drain up to 40% of our productivity. Think about it: you're knee-deep in debugging code, then boom, it's time for a short status meeting or internal short preparation meeting to plan another short meeting. Your brain shifts gears from deep, complex thinking to mundane meeting mode. It's like going from solving quantum physics to discussing the office coffee supply.

After a meeting, jumping back into your original task isn't like resuming a paused movie. It's more like reconstructing a puzzle blindfolded. You need to recall all the intricate details and threads of thought you had before being interrupted. This reactivation process is a time-consuming mental workout, often leading to forgotten nuances and increased errors, and it also has psychological impact.

Have you ever tried to move on to a new task but found your brain stubbornly clinging to the previous one? That's called "attention residue," where a part of your brain is still gnawing on the old task while you're trying to focus on the new one. It's like a bad song stuck in your head distracting and hard to shake off. This residue significantly hampers performance, especially when switching between tasks that require high cognitive load. You feel stressed and cognitive fatigue.

Frequent interruptions lead to a state of continuous partial attention, where you're spread so thin you can't fully focus on anything. It's like trying to have a meaningful conversation in the middle of a rock concert, which is super frustrating and exhausting. This constant state of alert not only reduces deep work capacity but also ramps up stress and cognitive fatigue, making it harder to perform effectively.

Consider a software engineer deep in the trenches, battling a critical bug. Each interruption pulls them out of their focused state, forcing them to attend to less pressing matters before diving back into the complex code. Each disruption delays bug resolution and ups the error count, setting the stage for more issues down the line.

In our quest for efficiency, we often pack meetings tightly together, believing that shorter equals better. But these rushed sessions usually end up being superficial, like skimming a book's table of contents and claiming you've read it. Participants feel pressured to blurt out their points without fully developing them, resulting in discussions that barely scratch the surface.

These hasty meetings become a revolving door of follow-ups, each more frustrating than the last. There's no time for probing questions or in-depth exploration, leaving participants with a sense of dissatisfaction. They know that given more time, the discussion could've led to significant breakthroughs.

Creativity thrives in environments where ideas can be discussed at length. You cannot discuss an idea on the fly and within few seconds or minutes. We must allot enough time to discuss the ideas. It's in these extended dialogues that innovative solutions often emerge. Short meetings, however, stifle this process. We feel rushed as we must ran off to another short meeting. And it is a never-ending loop. These short meetings eventually become a checklist exercise, sidelining creativity for the sake of expediency.

Rushed discussions not only impact immediate outcomes but also have long-term repercussions. Decisions made in haste are often based on incomplete information, leading to issues that require more time and resources to fix later. Plus, the chance to build trust and understanding through rich conversation is lost, affecting team cohesion and collaboration.

To mitigate these downsides, organizations should consider lengthening critical meetings, focusing on well-thought-out agendas that prioritize depth over breadth. Encourage an atmosphere where taking the time to delve into issues is valued. Facilitators can ensure all voices are heard and discussions are allowed to develop naturally, rather than being cut short by the clock.

So, next time you think a quick question or a short meeting will save time, remember: it's the quality of engagement that truly matters. Let's protect our cognitive flow and create spaces where real, meaningful collaboration can happen. As the saying goes: "An uninterrupted mind crafts masterpieces; a broken thought crafts mediocrity. Value time, cherish flow."

Contribution to Burnout: The High Cost of Constant Context-Switching

Let's face it, switching tasks every few minutes is like trying to have a meaningful conversation in the middle of a carnival. It's chaotic, exhausting, and downright unsustainable. In today's turbo-charged workplace, juggling multiple topics at once isn't just common; it's practically a sport. But this constant context-switching is a major culprit behind employee burnout, a stealthy villain that can derail both personal well-being and organizational health. We are having a cognitive overload.

Imagine your brain as a tiny circus performer spinning plates on sticks. Every time you switch tasks, you add another plate. Eventually, something's got to give. Each task-switch demands cognitive resources, and our brains, despite their brilliance, have limited bandwidth. This constant reallocation leads to cognitive overload, which not only tanks the quality of work but also fast-tracks mental fatigue. It's like trying to run a marathon while carrying a piano.

When we hop from task to task like caffeinated bunnies, our brains never get a chance to fully dive into any one thing. This shallow engagement means that the deeper cognitive processes essential for creativity and complex problem-solving are rarely fully engaged. Over time, our ability to solve problems and think innovatively shrinks faster than a wool sweater in hot water.

Constantly shifting gears isn't just mentally taxing; it's emotionally draining too. It leads to feelings of frustration, anxiety, and ultimately, disengagement. The stress of never feeling fully immersed or satisfied with one's work contributes to emotional exhaustion, a hallmark of burnout. Picture trying to read a book while someone flips the lights on and off every few seconds. That is super annoying, right? That's what our brains feel like with constant interruptions. There are evident long-term consequences on workplace morale and productivity.

Morale: Imagine trying to build a sandcastle while someone kicks it over every few minutes. Constant interruptions and the pressure to switch tasks can wreck team morale. When employees can't see tasks through to completion, it leads to a sense of inefficacy and demotivation. Every time they join those 15 minutes status meetings, that we have every day we feel super inefficient as we could not accomplish anything due to so many meetings in between, and if we do try to explain the reasons, then the management sees it just as an excuse. We then start feeling like hamsters on a wheel running fast but going nowhere.

Productivity: Here's the kicker: all this task-switching actually leads to decreased productivity. While it might seem like multitasking is the way to get more done, it's a trap. Energy is wasted just trying to keep up, resulting in rushed and lower-quality output. The cumulative effect of reduced quality and motivation can dramatically impact overall organizational productivity. It's like running on a treadmill expecting to reach a destination. Yes, some people, me included, thrive on multitasking, but there are limits.

Turnover and Institutional Knowledge: Burnout is a revolving door. Over time, it drives higher turnover rates, meaning not just the loss of talent but also a drain on institutional knowledge. This can stymie long-term innovation and growth. Plus, the costs of recruiting and training new employees to replace those who leave due to burnout add financial strain to the organization. It's like constantly bailing water out of a leaky boat instead of fixing the hole.

Organizations must recognize the dangers of relentless context-switching and take proactive steps to protect their most valuable asset and that is their people.

Companies must start designing workflows that allow for longer periods of focused work with fewer interruptions. This means fewer "urgent" drop-ins and more blocks of uninterrupted time. Think of it as letting the brain catch its breath.

We must implement scheduling practices that respect the need for deep work. Fewer, but more meaningful meetings with buffer times between different tasks can make a world of difference. It's like giving your brain a chance to stretch and warm up before the next sprint. Yes, it is totally ok for a person to have a whole day cleared of meetings.

We must try to develop a robust support systems that include access to mental health resources, regular check-ins with managers, and training programs that teach employees how to manage stress effectively. Support systems are the safety nets that catch you when the tightrope of work-life balance gets shaky. But we cannot complain, as that would be seen as bad and we would be seen as complainers. And nobody likes those.

In conclusion, by minimizing interruptions and fostering an environment conducive to deep work, organizations can significantly enhance both productivity and creativity. This approach not only benefits individual engineers but also contributes to the overall success and innovation capacity of the company. Let's stop treating our brains like circus performers and give them the respect and care they deserve. I cannot highlight that enough.

In my experience, I'm constantly being interrupted with short meetings from all departments; sales, marketing, customer meetings, product and project managers, development status updates. And guess what? I still need to create software!

Imagine my typical day, segmented into half-hour meetings, beginning with a project kickoff at 8:30 AM and ending with a wrap-up session at 5 PM. Between these, I attend various briefings, client updates, and team scrums. Each meeting, supposedly just 30 minutes long, often extends a few minutes over as each session invariably ends with, "Let's schedule another meeting to continue."

By lunchtime, I've switched contexts so many times that I barely recall details from my earlier discussions. The afternoon brings more of the same: fragmented conversations that demand switching mental gears without pause. By the end of the day, despite having been in continuous discussions, the tangible progress on projects is minimal. Critical tasks that require my attention are postponed, leading to delayed project milestones and mounting stress.

This scenario isn't unique to me; it mirrors a common experience across various industries where the proliferation of meetings can paradoxically stall productivity. The constant interruptions and context switches result in:

- **Project Delays:** Continuous partial attention spread across various meetings often leads to significant project hold-ups as deep work necessary for complex problem-solving is deferred.
- **Quality of Output:** The quality of work suffers as tasks receive less focused attention and more rushed execution in the limited gaps between meetings.
- **Employee Satisfaction:** The frustration of an unproductive day contributes to job dissatisfaction, with long-term implications for employee retention and morale.

We need to advocate for longer, and fewer, but more productive meetings. Longer meetings might seem counterintuitive in a culture that prizes brevity, but when planned thoughtfully, they can significantly enhance productivity. Extending meeting durations allows for more thorough discussions, reducing the need for follow-up meetings. With fewer but more focused meetings, each session can achieve deeper engagement and more definitive outcomes.

A well-prepared agenda is crucial for maximizing meeting efficiency. Effective agendas should:

- Clearly outline discussion points with allocated times.
- Specify objectives and expected outcomes for each item.
- Be circulated in advance to allow participants to prepare, ensuring a focused and productive discussion.

To respect employees' time and cognitive loads:

- Avoid scheduling back-to-back meetings. Incorporate buffer periods for employees to process information, take notes, and prepare for their next commitments.
- Designate certain days as meeting-free, allowing uninterrupted time for deep work.
- And please, let's stop using "everyone looks so busy, this was the only time found on everyone's calendar" as an excuse to overpack the day with short 30-minute meetings.

Cultivate a meeting culture that critically assesses the necessity of each meeting. Encourage alternatives such as:

- Detailed emails for updates that don't require immediate feedback.
- Quick calls for urgent decisions, but don't make every task and topic urgent.
- Asynchronous tools like shared documents for collaborative input that doesn't need real-time interaction.

In conclusion, meetings don't have to be the enemy of productivity. With a bit of strategic thinking and a dash of empathy for our cognitive limits, we can transform meetings from time-sucking monsters into effective, productive gatherings. And who knows? Maybe we'll finally have enough time left over to cook that perfect steak or at least debug that stubborn piece of code.

Conclusion: Rethinking Meetings for Greater Productivity and Well-being

Alright, folks, let's face it. Traditional meeting practices, especially the overuse of short, frequent "urgent" meetings, are not just inefficient but they're downright counterproductive. It's like trying to win a marathon by taking a nap every mile. The science behind task interruption and task switching gives us all the proof we need: we have to change how we handle meetings. If we restructure our approach, we can enhance productivity, employee satisfaction, and even innovation. Sounds like a win-win-win, right?

Adjusting meeting cultures is not just about moving some blocks around on your calendar; it's a strategic imperative. Frequent interruptions and the compulsion to switch tasks rapidly lead to cognitive overload. This stifles creativity and leads to burnout faster than you can say, "Let's schedule another quick meeting." By extending meeting durations and reducing their frequency, we can foster more meaningful engagement and thorough exploration of topics. This can help us avoid the endless loop of follow-up meetings and cut down the overall time spent in meeting rooms.

We need to challenge the current culture where everything is marked as critical and requires an immediate meeting. Here's a secret: not every task needs a meeting, and not every meeting needs to disrupt your workday. By critically evaluating the necessity of meetings and using alternative communication methods, such as detailed emails or quick calls, we can protect our time and cognitive resources.

Here's a practical step: designate specific days free from meetings, like "No Meeting Fridays." Imagine a day where you can actually focus on your tasks, catch up on work, and prepare for deadlines without the pressure of attending back-to-back meetings. This not only boosts productivity but also enhances job satisfaction. When employees feel their time and workflows are respected, everyone wins.

Ultimately, rethinking and restructuring meeting practices can lead to a more sustainable and productive work environment. This environment not only retains talent but also fosters a culture of well-being and high performance. As companies embrace these changes, they will see not just incremental but significant gains in productivity, creativity, and overall employee well-being.

It's time for leaders and managers to champion these changes. Let's advocate for a meeting culture that genuinely facilitates productivity rather than impedes it. By embracing these principles, we can ensure our operations align more closely with the needs and well-being of our workforce. Together, we can pave the way for a more effective and fulfilling professional environment.

So, here's to fewer, longer, and more meaningful meetings. Let's keep our sanity intact and make our workdays a little less chaotic. Cheers to productivity, well-being, and maybe even a little bit of peace and quiet!

Chapter 4

Empowering and Rewarding Great Engineering Talent

THE QUEST FOR EXCELLENCE

In the whirlwind world of technology, distinguishing between good and great engineers isn't just a luxury, it's a survival tactic. This chapter is your golden ticket to understanding why recognizing and nurturing top-tier talent is crucial for any organization that dreams of leading, innovating, and maybe even becoming the next big thing in the industry.

Let's face it: good engineers are the unsung heroes who keep the tech world turning. They're the ones you can count on to make sure everything works smoothly, day in and day out. But great engineers? They're the rockstars who can transform an ordinary company into something extraordinary. They don't just think outside the box, they often wonder why there was a box in the first place.

Imagine this: You're on a tight project deadline, and suddenly a new challenge pops up. A good engineer will solve the problem. A great engineer will solve it, then come up with five different ways to make sure it never happens again, and they'll make it look like a breeze. This kind of creative problem-solving and forward-thinking is what sets great engineers apart, making them invaluable assets to any company.

Why does distinguishing matter? Because it allows organizations to invest wisely. It's like knowing which plants in your garden are the perennials that will keep blooming year after year. By identifying and nurturing great engineers, you're ensuring those rare ideas not only sprout but flourish into groundbreaking products or solutions. In a field driven by rapid changes and high demands, the impact of a great engineer is like a ripple in a pond, exponential and far-reaching.

As we dive into this chapter, we'll explore the unique traits that set great engineers apart. We'll look at why it's essential to nurture and reward their talents and offer practical strategies to help transform your competent engineers into exceptional innovators. Because let's be honest, in a world where technology evolves faster than fashion trends, having a creatively empowered workforce isn't just a nice-to-have, it's a must-have.

So now we're about to embark on a quest for excellence. Whether you're an engineer or a manager, this chapter will give you the insights you need to recognize and cultivate greatness within your team.

Good vs. Great Engineers: Understanding the Distinction

What is the role of a good engineer? In essence it is consistency and reliability, and of course operational excellence.

Consistency and Reliability: Good engineers are the backbone of any tech operation. Think of them as the unsung heroes who keep the lights on, ensuring everything runs smoothly. They're like the steady heartbeat of a well-oiled machine, ensuring that day-to-day functions within a tech organization don't skip a beat. Their focus on consistency and reliability means you can set your watch by them, and they get the job done, every time. These engineers are the dependable ones you want around when you need a task executed with precision and adherence to established processes. In environments where predictability and stability are paramount, good engineers are the unsung heroes who bring everything together without a hitch.

Operational Excellence: When it comes to operational excellence, good engineers are the MVPs. They excel at maintaining the operational integrity of technology projects. They're like the meticulous chefs who ensure that every dish coming out of the kitchen is up to standard, day in and day out. Navigating set parameters, performing routine tasks with precision, and ensuring systems are both functional and efficient are all in a day's work for them. Their operational excellence is vital for keeping the basic gears of a company turning, providing the necessary groundwork upon which more innovative projects can be built.

Now, while the skills of good engineers are crucial, let's be real, technology isn't standing still, and neither should we. AI and automation are the game-changers of our era. You like it or not, it is here to stay. With these tools, many routine engineering tasks can be optimized or outright handled by intelligent systems. This doesn't mean our good engineers are out of a job, far from it. It just means the bar has been raised.

In this brave new world, good engineers are increasingly expected to go beyond merely executing tasks. They need to engage creatively with emerging technologies. Think of it as moving from being a line cook to a sous-chef who knows how to work the room and whip up a new dish when the mood strikes. Our good engineers need to learn how to harness AI tools to enhance their productivity and problem-solving capabilities. It's not about following orders anymore; it's about thinking outside the box and adding that unique human touch that AI just can't replicate.

While good engineers ensure stability and efficiency, there's a growing need for more creative and strategic thinking in everyday tasks. This is where the distinction between good and great engineers becomes particularly significant. Great engineers take their foundational skills and use them as a springboard to pioneer innovative solutions and lead transformative projects. Transitioning from good to great involves embracing challenges, thinking beyond the immediate, and continuously seeking improvement and innovation.

So, let's cheer for our good engineers as they are the solid foundation upon which everything else is built. But let's also encourage them to step into greatness, to leverage their skills in ways that not only meet today's demands but anticipate tomorrow's. Because in the ever-evolving landscape of technology, being technically proficient is just the beginning.

The Impact of Great Engineers

Great engineers don't just solve problems. They go beyond expectations. They redefine what's possible. They approach every task with a mindset that goes beyond merely getting the job done. Imagine them as the chefs or rock stars of the engineering world, always ready to turn the ordinary into extraordinary. They combine deep technical knowledge with a visionary outlook, often pioneering solutions that are both innovative and cost-effective. It's like having a chef who not only cooks a perfect steak but also invents a new cooking technique that revolutionizes the entire culinary industry. Their knack for exceeding expectations propels their organizations to the forefront of their industries.

- Innovative Problem Solving: Great engineers think outside the box, or sometimes, they throw the box away altogether. They apply unique, often risky solutions that can yield high rewards. This isn't just about having technical chops; it's about understanding business needs and market demands. Think of them as the Sherlock Holmes of engineering, always finding clues and solutions where others see dead ends.
- Application of AI and Automation: While some might see AI as a futuristic concept, great engineers are already using it to automate routine tasks, freeing up their brains for more complex challenges. It's like having a personal assistant who handles all the mundane stuff, so they can focus on the big, game-changing ideas. Their ability

to harness technology effectively lets them scale new heights in innovation.

In environments like cloud computing, where resources can be as elusive as a unicorn, great engineers show their mettle by optimizing costs without sacrificing performance. Their deep understanding of system architecture and proficiency in the latest tech allows them to design solutions that use resources efficiently. It's like having a magician who can pull not just one, but an entire bouquet of rabbits out of a hat without breaking a sweat.

- **Efficient Use of Technology:** By implementing sophisticated tools and using predictive analytics, they can manage resources proactively. It's like having a crystal ball that tells them when and where to allocate resources, preventing wastage and anticipating future needs.
- **Sustainable Practices:** Great engineers are also eco-warriors. They integrate sustainability into their architectural decisions, ensuring that their solutions are not only economically viable but also environmentally friendly. It's like building a skyscraper with recycled materials that is both cost-effective and green. Their focus on sustainability ensures that their innovations are scalable and can stand the test of time.

Great engineers are the secret sauce that turns a good organization into a great one. Their ability to think creatively, leverage advanced technologies, and optimize resources makes them invaluable assets. So, let's celebrate these engineering superheroes who continuously push the boundaries and redefine what's possible in the world of technology.

Great engineers don't just live in the moment, they've got one eye on the future and the other on making sure today's work doesn't bite us in the rear tomorrow. They have an eye on bigger picture, and are already a few steps ahead. They design and build solutions that are sustainable, scalable, and as future-proof as possible. You know, the kind of work that makes you go, "Wow, they really thought this through!"

- Forward Planning: Great engineers are like the chess grandmasters of tech. They're always thinking several moves ahead. They design systems with flexibility, anticipating future developments so we're not left scrambling to make major overhauls later. It's like they've got a crystal ball or something.
- Risk Management: These engineers are also part-time fortune tellers, foreseeing potential pitfalls and devising comprehensive strategies to avoid them. They develop contingency plans and implement robust security measures to safeguard against unforeseen events. Their proactive approach ensures that systems are resilient and capable of adapting to new challenges. Basically, they're the tech world's equivalent of a Swiss Army knife, prepared for anything.

Great engineers are strategic planners who ensure that today's solutions remain viable and effective in the future. Their long-term strategic thinking is integral to the success and sustainability of technological advancements, making them invaluable assets to any organization. They're not just solving today's problems; they're preemptively tackling tomorrow's.

Great engineers aren't just technical whizzes; they're also the kind of people you want to follow into battle, of course, only if that battle involves complex coding and innovative problem-solving. They inspire their peers and subordinates through their dedication, foresight, and creativity, cultivating a culture of continuous improvement and innovation.

- **Cultural Influence:** Great engineers create an environment where new ideas are welcomed and rigorously tested. They understand that innovation often comes from challenging the status quo and aren't afraid to push boundaries. In this open environment, failure is viewed not as a setback but as a valuable learning opportunity. This mindset encourages team members to experiment and explore new solutions without the fear of reprisal, leading to breakthrough innovations and improved processes.

- **Mentorship and Team Building:** Great engineers are like the Yodas of the tech world. Through active mentorship, they play a crucial role in developing the next generation of talent. They provide guidance and support, helping less experienced engineers to think critically and innovate freely. By sharing their knowledge and experience, they build strong, cohesive teams capable of tackling complex challenges. Their leadership style is collaborative and inclusive, promoting teamwork and collective problem-solving.

In essence, great engineers lead by example, demonstrating the qualities they wish to instill in others. They inspire their peers and subordinates to strive for excellence, fostering a culture that values creativity, continuous improvement, and resilience. This leadership not only enhances the immediate team's performance but also contributes to the long-term success and sustainability of the organization.

These rock stars of engineering continue to shape the future of technology and innovation, one brilliant idea at a time. They are the true visionaries, the ones who turn "what ifs" into "why nots" and push the boundaries of what's possible. Their blend of technical prowess, strategic foresight, and inspirational leadership makes them the superheroes of the tech world and are capable of turning routine tasks into extraordinary features.

Great engineers are not just technically adept; they also possess exceptional communication and empathy skills. These soft skills enable them to understand and integrate diverse perspectives, which fosters collaboration and innovation. Let's be honest, it's one thing to code a solution, but it's an entirely different ball game to explain that code to the marketing team without them dozing off.

By actively listening to the needs and challenges expressed by various departments, whether it's sales, marketing, or customer service, great engineers can craft solutions that align with the organization's broader goals. This holistic understanding ensures that the software they develop not only meets technical requirements but also supports the strategic objectives of different teams. Imagine translating "we need it to be faster" from marketing speak into actual performance improvements. It's almost like a superpower.

Empathy allows great engineers to put themselves in the users' shoes, designing solutions that are not only technically sound but also closely aligned with user needs and expectations. This sensitivity to the human aspect of technology ensures that the products they create are user-friendly, accessible, and capable of solving real-world problems. It's about making sure the app doesn't just work but works in a way that doesn't make users want to throw their devices out the window.

Great engineers' ability to communicate effectively and empathize with others helps them bridge the gap between technical and non-technical stakeholders. They can translate complex technical concepts into language that is easily understood by all members of an organization. This skill is crucial for facilitating better collaboration and decision-making. Think of it as being able to explain quantum physics using nothing but food analogies and everyone understands, and no one's left hungry for more information.

The combination of strong communication skills and empathy empowers great engineers to design solutions that are technically robust and deeply attuned to the needs and expectations of users and stakeholders. This approach fosters a more inclusive and innovative environment, driving continuous improvement and long-term success.

So, next time you marvel at a perfectly executed tech solution, remember it's not just about the code, it's about the people behind the code who listened, understood, and delivered with a touch of human brilliance. "A fine craftsman knows the value of both his tools and his talent."

Rewarding Excellence: Transforming Talent into Game-Changers

Recognizing and rewarding excellence in engineering isn't just about handing out paychecks; it's about creating an environment where innovation thrives, and talent transforms into game-changers. In high-skill environments, understanding what makes individuals tick is crucial for driving innovation. Recognition and rewards play a pivotal role, serving as both a means of compensation and a powerful motivational tool that boosts job satisfaction and loyalty.

Motivation through Incentives

Understanding human motivation, especially in environments that demand high skills, is essential for cultivating innovation. Financial incentives like profit sharing and stock options play a critical role in aligning an engineer's personal ambitions with the company's overarching goals. These rewards serve not only as a means of compensation but also as a significant motivational tool that enhances job satisfaction and loyalty.

- **Psychological Impact:** According to motivational theories such as Maslow's hierarchy of needs and Herzberg's two-factor theory, recognition and financial rewards fulfill the esteem needs critical for motivation at work. Just like getting a gold star in kindergarten, but with a bit more cash involved.

· **Risk and Reward:** By financially investing in their engineers, companies signal trust and confidence in their capabilities, encouraging them to undertake ambitious projects with potentially high rewards. It's like telling your engineers, "We believe in you! Now go build that next big thing... or at least don't blow up the server."

Partnership Opportunities

Offering shares or stakeholder status to high-performing engineers can transform them into true business partners. This level of trust and integration fosters a deep commitment to the company's long-term success and encourages a strategic approach to innovation.

· **Ownership Mentality:** When engineers stand to gain directly from the company's success, they are more likely to act in the best interests of the organization and think beyond their technical roles. It's amazing how much harder you work when it's your name on the line... or your potential yacht fund.
· **Sustained Engagement:** Ownership promotes sustained engagement and dedication, as engineers see their work contributing directly to their personal and professional growth. They're not just cogs in the machine; they're proud owners of the machine (and maybe a fancy new car someday).

Strategies to Nurture and Reward

Creating an Innovative Culture

Cultivating an environment where risk-taking and innovation are not just tolerated but celebrated is crucial for transforming good engineers into great ones. This involves creating a safe space for experimentation and, crucially, for occasional failure.

- **Celebrating Failure**: By acknowledging that failure is a natural part of pushing boundaries, companies can encourage their engineers to experiment boldly. This reduces the fear of repercussions and fosters a culture of continuous innovation. Remember, every great idea probably started as a not-so-great one.
- **Feedback Loops**: Establishing regular, constructive feedback loops helps reinforce positive behaviors and guide engineers toward successful outcomes. It's like having a GPS for your career, recalculating when you make a wrong turn, but always keeping you on the road to success.

Empowerment through Autonomy

Empowering engineers by granting them the autonomy to explore and implement their ideas can lead to significant breakthroughs. Autonomy is a powerful motivator as it taps into intrinsic motivations such as the desire for self-determination and mastery.

- **Trust in Expertise**: Autonomy shows trust in an engineer's skills and judgment, which boosts their confidence and willingness to undertake complex challenges. It's the ultimate vote of confidence: "We trust you. Go do your thing."
- **Customized Challenges**: Tailoring challenges to match the unique skills and interests of engineers can maximize their performance and satisfaction. Think of it as the professional version of setting the difficulty level on your favorite video game.

Structured Mentorship Programs

Developing structured mentorship programs where less experienced engineers can learn from seasoned innovators is crucial for nurturing talent and ensuring a continuous flow of knowledge and inspiration within the organization.

- **Knowledge Sharing**: Mentorship helps in the transfer of tacit knowledge that isn't easily acquired from books or formal training. It's the equivalent of passing down grandma's secret cookie recipe; priceless and delicious.
- **Role Modeling**: Mentors serve as role models, demonstrating the qualities and approaches that define great engineering. They show you the ropes and sometimes how to avoid hanging yourself with them.

Rewarding excellence goes beyond financial incentives. It includes opportunities for professional growth, such as advanced training, leadership roles, and challenging projects that push the boundaries of their skills. By offering these opportunities, companies demonstrate a commitment to their engineers' long-term career development.

In conclusion, recognizing and rewarding excellence transforms talented engineers into game-changers. By aligning personal ambitions with company goals and providing meaningful incentives, organizations create an environment where innovation thrives. This approach not only drives individual performance but also contributes to the overall success and competitive edge of the company.

By investing in these reward systems and supportive structures, companies not only enhance the capabilities of their current engineering teams but also lay the groundwork for a future where innovation and excellence are the norms. This strategy ensures that engineers are not only recognized for their efforts but are also encouraged to develop the fearlessness necessary to question, innovate, and lead in their fields. So, let's celebrate those engineers, not just for what they do, but for what they inspire us to become.

Conclusion: A Call to Action for Leaders

As we wrap up this chapter on the transformative power of recognizing and rewarding great engineering talent, it's crucial for leaders to understand the significant role they play in shaping their companies' futures. The ability of a tech-driven company to innovate and lead in its field depends heavily on the skills of its engineers. But even more so, it depends on how these skills are nurtured, developed, and appreciated.

One major mindset shift for today's corporate leaders is seeing expenditures on salaries, bonuses, and professional development for top engineering talent not as costs, but as significant investments. Think of it like this: you're not just paying for an engineer; you're investing in a source of innovation, efficiency, and competitive edge. It's like buying a golden goose, except instead of eggs, it lays groundbreaking technology.

Investing in top talent should be viewed through the lens of long-term value creation. Top engineers bring about breakthrough innovations and system optimizations that can save organizations substantial amounts of money or open up new revenue streams over time. Imagine having someone on your team who can not only fix today's problems but also create tomorrow's opportunities.

Beyond immediate financial incentives, investing in engineers' growth and satisfaction contributes to a more motivated, creative, and loyal workforce. This, in turn, reduces turnover rates, lowers recruitment costs, and builds a stronger organizational culture. Basically, happy engineers = a thriving company.

Leaders must challenge the prevailing business norms that treat human resource expenditures as mere numbers on a balance sheet. Instead, they should foster a culture of recognition and encourage risk-taking.

Cultivate an environment where exceptional talent is regularly recognized and rewarded, not just with financial benefits but also with opportunities for growth and expressions of trust. Let them lead key projects or participate in strategic decision-making. Remember, when you trust someone with responsibility, they tend to rise to the occasion.

By rewarding not just success but also the courage to innovate and experiment, companies can encourage a culture where taking calculated risks is seen as an essential path to discovery and improvement. Let's face it, if we never took risks, we'd still be lighting fires by rubbing sticks together instead of using a lighter.

Rethinking how engineering talent is treated is not just an HR concern; it is a strategic imperative. Companies that excel in attracting, developing, and retaining the best engineers will lead the future of technology and innovation. Leaders must act decisively to ensure that their organizations are not just participants but leaders in this dynamic technological era.

In empowering engineers, leaders validate their contributions, inspire their best work, and signal to the entire organization that striving for excellence is both recognized and rewarded. It is these empowered engineers who will not only meet the challenges of today but will also innovate and engineer the solutions of tomorrow. So, let's get out there, appreciate our engineers, and watch as they transform the world with their creativity and brilliance. As the proverb says: "A wise leader knows that the best way to lead is to empower others to shine."

Chapter 5

The Hidden Burden: Navigating the Pitfalls of Technical Debt

Welcome to the wild world of software development, where "technical debt" is the unwelcome guest that nobody invited but everyone has to deal with. It's like that pile of dirty dishes in your sink. You can ignore it for a while, but eventually, it's going to start smelling. This chapter is your guide to understanding what technical debt is, why it's a big deal, and how both engineers and project managers can play nice to manage it effectively. We will explore the often-overlooked impact of technical debt on software stability and scalability and propose strategies for effective management.

First things first, what exactly is technical debt? Imagine you're building a house, but you decide to use duct tape instead of nails because, hey, it's faster and cheaper. The house stands, but it's only a matter of time before things start falling apart. In software development, technical debt is the shortcut you take to meet deadlines or quickly roll out features, sacrificing code quality or system design in the process. Like financial debt, it incurs "interest"; the longer you wait to fix it, the more expensive and painful it becomes.

Technical debt can sneak up on you in various ways, much like that "quick question" from a colleague that turns into a 45-minute discussion. In this chapter we will delve deeper into the most common culprits like rushed releases, temporary fixes and legacy code. When you're up against the clock, corners get cut, and quality takes a back seat. It's like cramming for an exam and hoping for the best. You know those "temporary" solutions that end up sticking around forever? Yeah, those add up. And sometimes, you must work with ancient code that nobody dares to touch. It's the software equivalent of inheriting your grandma's old attic full of "treasures."

When a software system fails, it's like a game of hot potato, nobody wants to hold onto the blame. Managers may claim ignorance and they often claim they were in the dark about the technical shortcuts being taken. They might say things like, "I had no idea this was happening," while engineers, who are usually the ones patching things up, feel like they had no choice but to cut corners under tight deadlines. This creates a culture where engineers are hesitant to raise concerns about technical debt because it's like telling a toddler they can't have more candy, and let's face it, nobody wants to hear it.

Picture this: the system crashes, and suddenly everyone's running around like headless chickens. Managers are pointing fingers, and sometimes escalating without a need while engineers are scrambling to find the root cause, and somewhere in the chaos, there's an intern wondering if it's too late to switch careers. This blame game underscores the need for clear communication and shared responsibility. If everyone's on the same page from the start, managing technical debt proactively becomes a team effort rather than a last-minute scramble.

And it is understandable that engineers, who are often on the frontline, might feel they were left with no choice but to cut corners. They are forced to prioritize immediate functionality over long-term system integrity due to being under immense pressure to meet tight deadlines. As I mentioned before this pressure can lead to a workplace culture where raising concerns about increasing technical debt is not just discouraged but actively suppressed. Unfortunately voices that might advocate for a more sustainable approach to software development are often drowned out by the urgent demands of project schedules and delivery expectations.

So, how do we keep our software house from falling apart? Well, first and foremost, we need to foster a transparent communication. We have to ensure that everyone understands the trade-offs being made and the long-term impacts. It's like holding a family meeting about why eating cookies for dinner isn't sustainable. We must perform refactoring and dedicate time to clean up the codebase regularly. Think of it as spring cleaning for your software. And above all we must prioritize quality and encourage a culture where quality isn't just a checkbox but a core value. In the fast software development, we should strive to reward teams for sustainable solutions, not just quick fixes.

In the end, managing technical debt is about balance. It's okay to take shortcuts sometimes, but make sure you have a plan to pay off that debt before it spirals out of control. Remember, a well-placed line of code saves a thousand headaches later. So, let's roll up our sleeves, communicate openly, and tackle technical debt head-on, before it turns into a crisis that nobody wants to own.

Now that we have set the stage, let's dive into those various culprits that contribute to the technical debt that I've mentioned above. Just like that hidden pile of dishes you've been avoiding, these factors need to be addressed before they start to stink up the place.

Rushed Product Releases with Inadequate Refactoring or Testing

In the mad dash to meet market deadlines, essential stages of development like refactoring or comprehensive testing are often skipped. This can lead to the deployment of features that work superficially but have underlying issues in code quality and maintainability. Think of it as slapping a fresh coat of paint on a crumbling wall. It might look good at first, but it won't hold up.

The shortcuts taken during these rushed releases often result in bugs that are more difficult and costly to fix later. Without proper refactoring, the codebase can become cluttered and complex, making it hard for developers to navigate and update efficiently. It's like trying to find your way through a jungle with a butter knife, which is frustrating and ineffective.

Selection of Simpler, Quicker Solutions Over More Robust, Scalable Options

Under intense deadline or budget pressures, teams might opt for solutions that are easier and quicker to implement at the moment, rather than investing time in more robust and scalable options. This is like choosing fast food over a home-cooked meal, satisfying in the short term, but not great for long-term health.

Such choices may provide temporary relief but usually fail to accommodate future growth effectively. As the system scales, these "quick fixes" can lead to performance bottlenecks and increased maintenance challenges, requiring substantial rework to align with evolving business needs.

Legacy Systems Carrying Forward Outdated Code and Technologies

Many organizations rely on legacy systems that carry outdated code and technologies due to the high costs and risks associated with updating them. These systems often form the backbone of critical business operations, making disruptions undesirable. It's like driving a classic car; it looks cool, but good luck finding parts for it.

Legacy systems can significantly slow down innovation. They may not support newer technologies or methodologies, leading to a technological mismatch with new developments. Additionally, older code may not comply with current security standards, posing risks to the system's integrity and security.

Each of these sources of technical debt not only affects the technical quality of the product but also impacts the morale and productivity of the development team. Over time, dealing with the complications arising from these decisions can lead to developer frustration and reduced efficiency. Furthermore, the presence of significant technical debt can deter new talent from joining the organization, as they may be reluctant to work with outdated or overly complex systems.

The Non-Technical Stakeholder's Debt

One of the most challenging aspects of managing technical debt stems from the significant disconnect that often exists between technical teams and non-technical stakeholders. This gap can lead to serious misalignments that adversely affect the project's long-term viability.

Non-technical project and product managers often prioritize immediate deliverables that can be quickly demonstrated and appreciated in business terms, such as new features or user interfaces. These visible functionalities are frequently pushed to the forefront to meet short-term business goals or impress stakeholders, often at the expense of the underlying technical quality and sustainability of the project.

This focus on short-term visibility can lead non-technical managers to overlook the importance of investing time and resources in refactoring, updating dependencies, or addressing accumulated technical debt. As a result, the product may meet initial business expectations but suffer from increased maintenance costs and reduced flexibility in the long run.

Non-technical stakeholders often lack a deep understanding of the technical intricacies involved in software development. This can lead to a significant underestimation of the risks associated with technical debt, such as the potential for increased system outages, performance bottlenecks, and security vulnerabilities.

Because non-technical stakeholders may not see the immediate effects of neglecting technical debt, they might assume it is a manageable issue that can be deferred indefinitely. However, as technical debt accumulates, it can severely limit the system's ability to adapt to new requirements or scale efficiently, leading to costly overhauls down the line.

Bridging the Communication Gap

Now we will transition from identifying the issues to fixing them, and talk about how we can bridge the communication gap between technical and non-technical stakeholders to tackle technical debt effectively.

Educational Initiatives: It is crucial for technical leaders to take proactive steps to educate non-technical stakeholders about the implications of technical debt. This involves explaining technical challenges and debt-related risks in accessible, business-relevant terms. Regular presentations, reports, and real-time dashboards can help illustrate how technical debt could impact business objectives. Think of it as giving a crash course in "Tech Debt 101", making sure everyone speaks the same language.

Inclusive Decision-Making: Integrating non-technical stakeholders into the technical planning process can help align their expectations with the realities of software development. This integration helps ensure that decisions about feature prioritization, deadlines, and resource allocation consider both business needs and technical health. It's like inviting them to the kitchen to see why you can't just whip up a gourmet meal in five minutes.

We need to advocate for a balanced approach. Engineers and technical managers must be empowered to advocate for the importance of addressing technical debt. They need to make a compelling case that while innovation is critical, the long-term stability and efficiency of the product are equally important. Essentially, it's about making sure everyone knows that you can't keep driving a car with a flat tire and expect it to perform well.

Engineering leaders should work with business managers to set realistic timelines and project scopes that allow for the necessary work on reducing technical debt without sacrificing the product's technical integrity. This is akin to ensuring you have enough time to bake the cake properly rather than serving a half-baked mess.

The Impact of Technical Debt: Building on Shaky Foundations

Accumulating technical debt in software development can be likened to constructing a house of cards: while rapid progress might seem achievable in the short term, the lack of a robust structural foundation can lead to inevitable collapse under pressure. This analogy vividly illustrates how technical debt, often invisible in early project stages, can culminate in significant challenges as it builds up. Here, we delve deeper into the far-reaching consequences of neglected technical debt in terms of increased costs and reduced agility.

Just as a house of cards becomes increasingly unstable and difficult to repair with each added layer, software with high technical debt sees escalating costs for modifications and maintenance. The longer the debt remains unaddressed, the more expensive it becomes to implement changes, not merely due to the complexity of intertwined poor-quality code but also due to the accumulated dependencies that must be untangled.

In crisis situations, the cost of making emergency fixes can be exorbitant, often requiring extensive resources to stabilize the system swiftly. High technical debt severely restricts a team's ability to adapt to new market demands or technological advancements. Like a rigid structure that cannot be easily modified without risking collapse, software systems burdened with debt lack the flexibility to integrate new features or scale efficiently.

The focus shifts from innovation to managing crises and patches, which stifles creative problem-solving and prolongs development cycles. Systems riddled with technical debt are prone to frequent failures, much like a house of cards that topples at the slightest nudge. These failures can range from minor glitches to catastrophic crashes, each eroding user trust and satisfaction.

When failures occur at critical moments, the impact extends beyond technical setbacks to include significant business losses and reputational damage. Now, what is the role of great engineers in managing and addressing technical debt?

The Role of Great Engineers in Addressing Technical Debt

We have identified various sources of technical debt, and now we are transitioning to shining a spotlight on the real heroes of our story: great engineers and how they tackle technical debt like the seasoned pros they are.

Great engineers stand at the forefront of tackling technical debt, playing a critical role that extends beyond mere technical duties. These folks are like the Gandalf of the coding world, standing firm against the encroaching darkness of technical debt. Their responsibilities include not only identifying and quantifying the extent of technical debt but also effectively communicating its long-term implications to both technical and non-technical stakeholders.

Great engineers are the custodians of code quality and system integrity. They champion the adoption of sustainable development practices, understanding that the true measure of software success lies in its quality and maintainability, not merely its functionality. This involves advocating for practices such as regular code reviews, comprehensive testing procedures, and the incorporation of time for addressing technical debt into project schedules. By promoting these best practices, great engineers ensure that the software not only meets the current needs but also remains robust and flexible for future enhancements.

One of the significant challenges that great engineers face is bridging the understanding gap between the engineering team and non-technical stakeholders, such as project managers and business executives. This task involves translating complex technical issues into clear, impactful business terms. Great engineers must articulate how technical debt can lead to increased costs, reduced system performance, and potential downtimes that could affect business operations and customer satisfaction. They must explain that unresolved technical debt can escalate into critical failures at inopportune times, potentially leading to severe business repercussions.

It's crucial for great engineers to not only voice their concerns but also to document these interactions meticulously. This documentation ensures that there is a record showing that potential risks were communicated, which can be vital for accountability and future reference, especially when decisions to override engineering advice lead to system issues.

For great engineers, being vocal about technical debt is not just about pointing out problems but about fostering a culture where long-term system health is a priority. While they might sometimes be overridden by business priorities, their persistent advocacy and educational efforts can gradually shift organizational perspectives toward valuing technical sustainability as much as immediate business outcomes. Even if initially overlooked, consistent and reasoned communication from engineers about the dangers of technical debt can lead to a gradual shift in how decisions are made at higher levels.

Organizations that empower their engineers to speak up and take part in strategic decisions can mitigate risks more effectively. This empowerment helps in cultivating an organizational culture that values and acts upon the input from its technical experts.

Effectively managing and mitigating technical debt is crucial for maintaining the health and agility of software systems. It requires a multi-faceted approach that involves the entire organization, from the engineering teams to top management. Below are comprehensive strategies to manage technical debt effectively.

Creating an Environment of Transparency

Creating an environment where technical debt is regularly discussed and understood by all stakeholders is vital. This approach involves:

- **Open Dialogue:** Encourage ongoing conversations about technical debt within the development team and across different departments. This transparency helps in recognizing and addressing technical debt before it becomes critical.
- **Clear Business Implications:** Educate stakeholders about how technical debt impacts not only the development process but also business outcomes such as customer satisfaction, operational efficiency, and financial performance.
- **Regular Reporting:** Implement routine reporting mechanisms where updates on the status of technical debt are shared with both technical and non-technical team members, ensuring everyone understands the stakes involved.

Dedicated Remediation Efforts

Incorporating specific actions to reduce technical debt within regular development cycles can significantly alleviate its impact.

- **Allocate Time During Development Sprints:** Allocate time during development sprints specifically for refactoring and improving the codebase. This planned approach ensures that improvements are continuous and manageable.
- **Keep Documentation Up to Date:** Keep documentation up to date as part of the debt reduction efforts. Accurate documentation supports ongoing maintenance efforts and reduces the onboarding time for new team members.
- **Strengthen Quality Assurance Practices:** Strengthen quality assurance practices to include the identification and remediation of potential technical debt areas before new code is deployed.

Automated Tools and Processes

Leveraging technology can enhance the ability to manage technical debt effectively.

- **Code Analysis Tools:** Use automated tools to scan and identify problematic areas in the code. These tools can help prioritize which parts of the system need urgent refactoring based on potential risk.
- **Debt Tracking:** Implement systems to track and quantify technical debt, much like tracking financial debt. This quantification can help in prioritizing debt reduction tasks based on their potential impact on the business.
- **Integration into CI/CD Pipelines:** Integrate these tools into Continuous Integration/Continuous Deployment

(CI/CD) pipelines to ensure that technical debt considerations are part of every build and deployment process.

Developing a shared understanding of technical debt across the organization is essential for its effective management:

- **Educational Workshops:** Conduct workshops and training sessions for all stakeholders, explaining the concepts of technical debt, its causes, and its consequences.
- **Collaborative Problem Solving:** Encourage cross-functional teams to collaborate on identifying and solving technical debt issues. This cooperation can lead to innovative solutions that are beneficial from both technical and business perspectives.
- **Cultural Shift:** Foster a culture that values long-term code health as much as short-term achievements. This cultural shift can transform how technical debt is perceived and handled across the organization.

By implementing these strategies, organizations can transform the way they handle technical debt, turning what is often an overlooked burden into an opportunity for improvement and innovation. This proactive management not only ensures the technical robustness of the product but also aligns it with business goals, creating a resilient and responsive business environment.

Conclusion: A Call to Strategic Action

Managing technical debt is not just a challenge for the engineering team to handle while everyone else kicks back with their feet up. It's a strategic imperative that demands the attention of everyone from the interns all the way up to the CEO. We need to understand the real costs associated with ignoring this ticking time bomb, not just in terms of immediate financial outlays, but also considering the long-term impacts on system stability and our beloved company's reputation.

To keep our innovation train chugging along without derailing, it's crucial for managers to get off their thrones and actively engage with the engineering teams. This engagement fosters a culture where technical considerations are not dismissed like that salad option on the menu. Managers need to be open to listening, and I mean really listening and understanding the technical gibberish that engineers talk about. This understanding is vital when planning project timelines and setting realistic customer expectations about new features and updates. Remember, a happy engineer is a productive engineer, and that's a win for everyone.

Managers also need to sharpen their pencils when making promises to customers. These commitments should come with a clear understanding of the technical debt lurking in the background. By aligning customer expectations with the software's current state and the technical work required, managers can avoid the dreaded overpromise and underdeliver scenario. Trust me, nothing ruins a relationship faster than promising a five-star experience and delivering a soggy, two-star mess.

It's imperative that both engineering insights and managerial foresight guide the development process. This double whammy ensures that quality and long-term system health are not sacrificed for short-term gains. By valuing these aspects equally, organizations can strike a balance between meeting immediate business needs and ensuring the software's viability and competitiveness in the long term. Think of it as a seesaw where both sides need to be in sync to keep the ride enjoyable.

Finally, the entire organization must embrace a culture where quality, stability, and long-term planning are part of the daily grind, not just afterthoughts when things go sideways. This cultural shift ensures that technical debt management becomes a key component of everyday operations, rather than an emergency fix-it task. By adopting these strategic actions, companies can safeguard their technological infrastructure, boost their market position, and ensure continued growth and success.

So, let's roll up our sleeves, put on our thinking caps, and tackle technical debt head-on. Remember, managing technical debt isn't just about fixing what's broken; it's about building a future that's stable, innovative, and downright awesome. As the proverb goes "An ounce of prevention is worth a pound of cure."

Chapter 6

The Architect of Success: Why Great Engineers Are Essential for Your Team

So, now that we've hiked through the jungle of technical debt, let's pivot to something just as crucial: our engineering heroes who prevent these messes from even happening in the first place.

Following our exploration of technical debt, it becomes clear that the presence of great engineers, those who blend the roles of developers and architects, is crucial for the sustainability and success of software projects. While good engineers competently follow directions, great engineers challenge norms, question priorities, and steer projects toward both short-term wins and long-term stability.

Great engineers are much more than adept coders; they are pivotal strategists whose understanding of both the minute details and the overarching business implications of software development profoundly shapes the trajectory of projects. Their role involves far-reaching responsibilities that go beyond simple code creation to ensure that the projects they work on are not only successful in the short term but are sustainable and adaptable for future needs.

They stand as guardians of technical integrity, often challenging short-sighted decisions that could lead to the accumulation of technical debt. They advocate passionately for development practices that prioritize product stability and scalability over rushed or makeshift solutions. Their advocacy is crucial in environments where the pressure to deliver quickly can often lead to compromises that undermine the long-term health of the software.

One of the critical roles of great engineers is to provide comprehensive architectural oversight. They ensure that the architecture of a project is not just sufficient for current requirements but is robust and flexible enough to support future growth and changes. This foresight prevents projects from becoming obsolete or difficult to update as market demands evolve, ensuring that the software remains competitive and relevant.

With their deep technical insight and business acumen, great engineers play a vital role in the prioritization process within project management. They have a unique capability to assess and guide the prioritization of features and tasks, focusing on those that maximize the project's overall health and deliver significant business value. Their strategic input ensures that resources are allocated efficiently and that the development efforts align closely with the strategic goals of the organization.

Navigating Business and Technical Realities

We must acknowledge that great engineers excel at navigating the delicate intersection of business objectives and technical requirements. By effectively communicating the implications of technical decisions to non-technical stakeholders, they facilitate a deeper understanding and appreciation of the engineering challenges involved in software development. This role is critical in ensuring that business strategies are informed by technical realities, fostering an environment where decisions are made with a balanced perspective that values both immediate outcomes and long-term success.

In the swiftly evolving landscape of software development, the traditional role of project managers is increasingly questioned, particularly as many of their responsibilities overlap with those of senior or lead engineers. As technical teams become more autonomous and engineers gain skills in strategic planning and client communication, the necessity for project managers as middle managers may appear to diminish.

However, project managers still play a crucial role in bridging the gap between technical teams and business stakeholders, ensuring that project goals align with business objectives and managing resources across multiple projects. Their expertise in project tracking, risk management, and cross-functional coordination is invaluable in complex environments. We will explore this dynamic in detail in an upcoming chapter, examining how the roles of project managers are evolving and what future they might hold in the tech industry.

Navigating Pressures from Non-Technical Stakeholders

In the fast-paced environment of software development, project and product managers frequently face intense pressure from upper management and sales teams to deliver products quickly. This urgency often prioritizes speed over the technical health of the project, risking the creation of software that might meet immediate goals but fails to uphold standards of quality and scalability in the long term. In this high-stress landscape, the role of great engineers is paramount in steering projects toward successful outcomes without compromising the integrity of the software.

Great engineers possess the unique ability to balance the demand for rapid delivery with the critical need for robust and scalable solutions. They understand that quick fixes and shortcuts can lead to significant technical debt, potentially crippling the software in the future. By advocating for suffi-cient time to design and implement solutions properly, they ensure that the software not only functions effectively upon release but also remains maintainable and adaptable to future needs. Their technical expertise enables them to propose optimizations that reduce development time without sacrific-ing quality, presenting a balanced approach that satisfies both immediate project deadlines and long-term project health.

Another crucial function that great engineers serve is educat-ing non-technical stakeholders about the potential long-term consequences of neglecting technical health. They articulate these implications in terms that are relevant to business out-comes, such as the increased cost of maintenance, the risk of system failures, and the potential loss of customer trust that can arise from unstable or insecure software. By aligning the development team's strategies with the broader business objectives, great engineers help ensure that decisions regard-ing the project's scope and timeline consider both technical and commercial perspectives.

The recommendations and estimates provided by great engi-neers are deeply valued for their precision and foresight. With extensive experience and a comprehensive understanding of both the technical landscape and the market environment, these engineers provide insights that are crucial for informed decision-making. Their ability to forecast potential issues and propose proactive solutions earns them the trust and respect of project stakeholders, allowing them to influence key project decisions effectively. This trust is instrumental in ensuring that their voice is heard and heeded, particularly when they advocate for necessary adjustments or highlight risks that might not be immediately apparent to non-technical team members.

By fulfilling these roles, great engineers act as both safeguards and catalysts within their projects, ensuring that the drive for quick results does not undermine the software's functionality and viability in the long run. Their involvement is critical in aligning technical strategies with business goals, thereby enhancing the overall success and sustainability of software projects.

The influence of great engineers extends well beyond the technical aspects of a project. They play a transformative role in shaping team dynamics, cultivating a culture that aspires to excellence and continuous improvement. Through their actions and attitudes, these pivotal figures set benchmarks that elevate the entire team's performance and mindset.

Great engineers possess an unwavering commitment to quality, which establishes a high standard of excellence within the team. This commitment permeates through every phase of a project, influencing others to adhere to similarly high standards. Their approach goes beyond mere compliance with technical specifications; it involves a holistic view of what quality means, from clean, maintainable code to user-centric design. By setting such standards, they create an environment where excellence is the norm rather than the exception, fostering a culture where every team member is encouraged to strive for the best in every task they undertake.

Beyond their direct contributions, great engineers have a profound impact on the development of their colleagues. Through mentoring, they share valuable insights and experiences that elevate the team's overall capabilities. This mentoring is not limited to formal sessions but often occurs organically during collaborative work, code reviews, or problem-solving sessions. By actively sharing their knowledge and skills, great engineers help others to understand complex concepts and apply best practices in their work, thereby enhancing the collective competency of the team.

Great engineers are characterized by their willingness to question established norms and explore new possibilities. This trait is crucial for innovation, which can manifest in numerous forms, not just through groundbreaking products but also through incremental improvements, process enhancements, or novel approaches to problem-solving. Their drive for innovation encourages a mindset of creative thinking and experimentation within the team. It challenges everyone to think differently and to consider new ways of achieving goals, which can lead to innovations that significantly advance the project or the organization's overall offerings.

Conclusion: Investing in Engineering Excellence

Investing in great engineers goes far beyond merely filling a role; it represents a profound strategic commitment to the future of your projects and the overall success of your organization. These individuals are not just developers; they are creators and innovators whose broad skills and deep insight into both technology and business make them invaluable in navigating complex project landscapes.

Great engineers serve as stewards of current project viability and are crucial drivers of future innovation. Their ability to advocate for technically sound practices and influence project trajectories makes them indispensable in ensuring that development efforts align with long-term strategic goals. These talents bring a level of expertise and vision that can transform ordinary projects into extraordinary successes, thereby significantly enhancing your organization's competitive edge in the marketplace.

Therefore, when you encounter truly excellent engineers, it becomes imperative to do everything possible to retain and support them. Their presence not only stabilizes and enriches your projects but also acts as a catalyst for fostering a culture of excellence and innovation within your team. By viewing great engineers as vital investments rather than costs, companies can unlock remarkable potential and achieve sustained success in an increasingly competitive and dynamic industry landscape. As the proverb says "Invest in people, and they will invest in you."

Chapter 7

Navigating Office Politics: A Barrier to Engineering Innovation

In our discussions of what drives great engineers, we've acknowledged the critical importance of recognizing and nurturing their technical competence. Now, I want us to dive into a less glamorous but equally vital aspect of the workplace: office politics, and how it can negatively affect the engagement and retention of top engineering talent. Grab your popcorn as this is going to get interesting.

At many organizations, there's a constant tug-of-war between visionary executive strategies and grounded engineering expertise. Think of it as a corporate soap opera: the dreamers vs. the doers. Great engineers are innovators by nature, dedicated to precision, logical decision-making, and solutions grounded in data and proven methodologies. But they frequently encounter conflicts with decision-makers who sometimes seem to live in a parallel universe where everything is "just a minor tweak away" from perfection.

Imagine a typical day where I'm in a meeting discussing a new project. The executives outline this grand vision, which is something straight out of a sci-fi movie. As the engineering team, we start pointing out potential pitfalls, technical challenges, and the need for realistic timelines. But somewhere in the middle of translating this vision through various managerial layers, things get murky. Middle managers, who are often tasked with bridging these worlds (technical and business), but yet sometimes these middle managers are becoming the very barriers that stall progress.

Sometimes, the grand visions set by executives get lost in translation. Picture a game of telephone: the message starts as "build a scalable, secure platform" and ends up as "we need it done by Friday, and can it make coffee too?" Middle managers, not fully grasping the strategic nuances or the technical intricacies, can lead to diluted or skewed execution plans that fail to encapsulate the original intent. And more often than not they want to score some extra bonus points with the executives so they overpromise.

Middle managers often come from diverse backgrounds and may not have the technical depth needed for certain projects. This can result in decisions that prioritize quick wins or superficial metrics over technical integrity and long-term viability. It's like asking a chef to build a house. Sure, they can make it look nice, but will it stand the test of time?

Under intense pressure to deliver quickly, middle managers might prioritize immediate business objectives at the expense of technical integrity. It's like building a house of cards: it might look impressive for a moment, but it won't take much to bring it down.

On top of all these "misunderstandings" micromanagement and control comes into the picture. Micromanagement can really stifle creativity and problem-solving capabilities. It's like trying to paint a masterpiece with someone constantly adjusting your brush. Engineers need space to innovate, not a detailed checklist on how to think. Unfortunately, lots of managers are creating and following their own detailed checklist without consulting with engineers.

Promoting Compliance Over Expertise

And this is where the rubber hits the road. The clash between direction and expertise often leads to favoring engineers who agree with management. That's where good engineers come into the picture, and we've discussed those. Now, let's dive deeper into this conundrum.

In many companies, the progression and recognition of employees often hinge more on their compliance with managerial directives than on their capacity to innovate and challenge the status quo. This preference for alignment over questioning can foster a workplace culture where 'yes-men' are more likely to ascend the corporate ladder than true innovators.

Let me share a story that illustrates this perfectly. Picture this: a few years back, in the midst of a major project, we had two engineers. Let's call them John and Jane. John was a textbook example of a 'yes-man'. He nodded along in meetings, never questioned directives, and was quick to implement whatever was asked of him, no matter how impractical it seemed. Jane, on the other hand, was the embodiment of innovation. She would frequently challenge the status quo, propose new solutions, and wasn't afraid to voice her concerns, even if it meant ruffling a few feathers.

During a pivotal project meeting, Jane proposed a radical redesign of our system architecture that promised significant long-term benefits but required a considerable upfront investment of time and resources. As she laid out her plan, complete with detailed projections and potential risks, I noticed the usual suspects around the table, the managers, begin to fidget. One of them finally spoke up, "Jane, this is impressive, but maybe we should stick to what we know works. We can take this some other time in the future when we have more time and resources."

John, ever the agreeable one, chimed in, "I agree. We should stick to our current plan." And just like that, Jane's groundbreaking idea was shelved.

Months later, the project hit a critical snag. The system's limitations, which Jane had foreseen, started causing significant issues. We were scrambling, putting out fires, and the dreaded technical debt was piling up. It was a mess, and everyone knew it.

One day, after a particularly brutal meeting where we discussed yet another workaround to the system's growing problems, Jane pulled me aside. "You know," she said with a wry smile, "I feel like that guy who tried to sell umbrellas in the desert, only for it to start raining cats and dogs the next day."

Imagine proposing a groundbreaking solution in a meeting only to be met with blank stares and a polite, "Let's stick to what we know." This approach can lead to a significant loss of innovative capabilities, as the organization slowly devolves into an echo chamber of outdated practices. It's like trying to cook a gourmet meal in a kitchen where the only ingredients allowed are salt and pepper. Even those two ingrediencies are great, but let's face it, it is bland and uninspiring. You have probably noticed by now that I like to compare software engineering with cooking, and engineers with chefs. Well, I just love to cook and create.

It's easy to see how such a culture stifles creativity and innovation. The focus shifts from finding the best solution to finding the easiest path to approval. This not only demoralizes those who are willing to push boundaries but also leads to a homogenous group of thinkers who rarely challenge the status quo.

Let me take you on another journey, this time, a more hopeful one. In a different company, I once worked with a manager named Lisa. Well, we call her Lisa for the story's sake. She was new to the role but brought with her a refreshing perspective on leadership. Lisa valued expertise over compliance and made it clear from day one.

One day, during a meeting, an engineer named Mike proposed a new method for optimizing our database queries. It was a complex solution that required significant changes to our existing processes. As expected, there were some raised eyebrows and hesitant glances around the room.

But instead of shutting him down, Lisa asked Mike to explain his idea in detail. She did not schedule short half an hour meeting to understand the proposal. She facilitated a discussion where everyone could weigh in, ensuring that all voices were heard, and she allotted more than enough time. After a thorough evaluation, Lisa decided to give Mike's idea a shot, despite the initial resistance.

The results were astonishing. Mike's approach not only improved our system's performance but also sparked a wave of innovation across the team. People felt empowered to share their ideas, knowing they would be given fair consideration. It was a turning point that transformed our work culture.

Addressing the Culture of Compliance

Companies must start valuing the dissenting voices that challenge inefficiencies and propose improvements. Leadership training should include strategies for fostering an inclusive culture that welcomes debate and values different viewpoints. This not only enriches the decision-making process but also bolsters employee engagement and loyalty.

To address the culture of compliance, organizations can take several steps:

1. **Empower Expertise:** Encourage engineers to participate in strategic discussions and decision-making processes.
2. **Educate Managers:** Provide training to middle managers to enhance their understanding of technical challenges.
3. **Foster Open Communication:** Establish clear channels for engineers to voice concerns and recommendations without fear of reprisal.
4. **Value Long-Term Gains:** Shift focus from short-term achievements to long-term sustainability and innovation.
5. **Promote Diverse Viewpoints:** Encourage a multidisciplinary approach to problem-solving, integrating diverse perspectives for more innovative solutions.

By implementing these strategies, organizations can create a more dynamic and innovative environment, where true expertise is valued over mere compliance. This not only leads to better project outcomes but also fosters a culture of continuous improvement and excellence.

Navigating Pressures from Non-Technical Stakeholders

In the fast-paced environment of software development, project and product managers frequently face intense pressure from upper management and sales teams to deliver products quickly. This urgency often prioritizes speed over the technical health of the project, risking the creation of software that might meet immediate goals but fails to uphold standards of quality and scalability in the long term.

Great engineers possess the unique ability to balance the demand for rapid delivery with the critical need for robust and scalable solutions. They understand that quick fixes and shortcuts can lead to significant technical debt, potentially crippling the software in the future. By advocating for sufficient time to design and implement solutions properly, they ensure that the software not only functions effectively upon release but also remains maintainable and adaptable to future needs.

Let me take you back to a particularly stressful period in my career. Our team was working on a crucial project with an impossible deadline. Upper management was breathing down our necks, and the sales team had already promised the moon to our clients, as they always do and then disappear when implementation is support to start. It felt like we were on a sinking ship with no lifeboats in sight.

One day, in a meeting that was supposed to be a quick update but dragged on forever (as they do), our lead engineer, Tom, suggested a solution that would ensure long-term stability but would take an extra two weeks. The room went silent. You could hear the collective gulp of the managers and the account executives. Then, our project manager, with a look that could freeze lava, said, "Tom, we don't have two weeks. We need this done yesterday."

Tom, calm and composed, replied, "I understand the urgency, but if we rush this, we're going to spend double the time fixing bugs later. Remember the fiasco with Project Speedy? Let's not repeat that."

Everyone remembered Project Speedy, the project that was supposed to revolutionize our product line but ended up being a costly nightmare due to hastily implemented features. Tom's mention of it made everyone pause. In that moment, the value of balancing speed and quality became crystal clear. We eventually took Tom's advice, and while the extra time was a tough sell, the end result was a stable, scalable solution that didn't crumble under pressure. And sometimes we do need those extra couple of weeks.

Another crucial function that great engineers serve is educating non-technical stakeholders about the potential long-term consequences of neglecting technical health. They articulate these implications in terms that are relevant to business outcomes, such as the increased cost of maintenance, the risk of system failures, and the potential loss of customer trust that can arise from unstable or insecure software.

I recall another instance where I had to explain to our sales VP why refactoring was necessary. I used a simple analogy: "Imagine your car's engine is making a strange noise. You can either fix it now, which costs time and money, or ignore it until the engine fails completely, which will be far more expensive and disruptive." It was like a light bulb went off in his head. From then on, he was more receptive to our technical needs.

The recommendations and estimates provided by great engineers are deeply valued for their precision and foresight. With extensive experience and a comprehensive understanding of both the technical landscape and the market environment, these engineers provide insights that are crucial for informed decision-making. Their ability to forecast potential issues and propose proactive solutions earns them the trust and respect of project stakeholders. Please note that I am constantly referring to great engineers, not merely senior engineers. Experience alone doesn't make one great; it can make someone good. Greatness in engineering transcends years on the job; it is about innovation, leadership, and strategic thinking.

The influence of great engineers extends well beyond the technical aspects of a project. They play a transformative role in shaping team dynamics, cultivating a culture that aspires to excellence and continuous improvement.

Great engineers possess an unwavering commitment to quality, which establishes a high standard of excellence within the team. This commitment influences others to adhere to similarly high standards, fostering a culture where excellence is the norm.

Through mentoring, great engineers share valuable insights and experiences that elevate the team's overall capabilities. This mentoring often occurs organically during collaborative work, code reviews, or problem-solving sessions, enhancing the collective competency of the team.

Great engineers are characterized by their willingness to question established norms and explore new possibilities. This drive for innovation encourages a mindset of creative thinking and experimentation within the team, leading to groundbreaking products, process enhancements, or novel approaches to problem-solving.

Investing in great engineers goes far beyond merely filling a role; it represents a profound strategic commitment to the future of your projects and the overall success of your organization. These individuals are not just developers; they are creators and innovators whose broad skills and deep insight into both technology and business make them invaluable in navigating complex project landscapes.

Therefore, when you encounter truly excellent engineers, it becomes imperative to do everything possible to retain and support them. Their presence not only stabilizes and enriches your projects but also acts as a catalyst for fostering a culture of excellence and innovation within your team.

By viewing great engineers as vital investments rather than costs, companies can unlock remarkable potential and achieve sustained success in an increasingly competitive and dynamic industry landscape.

Conclusion: Building a Politically Healthy Workspace

If a company or an organization is serious about retaining top engineering talent and fostering innovation, tackling the negative impacts of office politics is crucial. But let's face it, this isn't just about reducing the drama, it's about tapping into the full potential of the team to drive collective success.

For companies truly aiming to leverage the brilliance of their engineering teams and secure a competitive edge, creating a politically healthy workspace is indispensable. Addressing office politics isn't just about keeping the peace; it's about valuing and integrating the expertise of engineers into the broader decision-making process.

By valuing and integrating the expertise of engineers into broader decision-making processes, companies can improve both employee satisfaction and the overall success of their projects.

Picture this: When engineers are involved in strategic discussions, it doesn't just improve project outcomes. It also boosts employee satisfaction by showing genuine respect and appreciation for their contributions. When engineers see their ideas influencing company strategies, it ignites their motivation and fosters a sense of ownership and commitment to organizational goals.

Creating a politically healthy workspace is about unlocking the collective success of the team. This requires leadership to promote transparency, encourage open communication, and cultivate an environment where diverse perspectives aren't just heard but actively integrated into the decision-making process. This way, every team member, regardless of their role, is aligned and moving towards a shared vision. This alignment is crucial for driving innovation and maintaining long-term success in an increasingly competitive industry.

By prioritizing these values, companies can not only retain top engineering talent but also transform their work environments into hubs of innovation and productivity. This isn't just a strategic move; it's a vital investment in the future of the organization. In a politically healthy workspace, the path to project success and overall business viability becomes clear and achievable.

We must at least try to create a workspace where political health translates directly into success, ensuring that everyone's potential is harnessed to its fullest, driving us all towards a brighter, more innovative future.

Chapter 8

Bridging Silos: Overcoming Inter-Team Conflicts in Engineering

In the multifaceted world of engineering, overcoming technical challenges is only part of the battle. The real hurdle? Inter-team conflicts. It's like trying to row a boat while everyone paddles in different directions. Whether it's differing methodologies, competition for resources, or the pursuit of recognition, these conflicts can seriously stymie collaboration and innovation. Despite all teams sharing the overarching goal of organizational success, these conflicts can create barriers that diminish overall productivity and morale.

Inter-team conflicts are not just surface-level disagreements; they often reflect deep-seated differences in operational methods and perspectives. These conflicts can significantly impede collaboration and overall progress, especially when not addressed thoughtfully. Let me tell you, these are the real-life

"Game of Thrones" episodes of the corporate world, complete with power plays, alliances, and the occasional backstabbing.

Imagine a project kickoff meeting where one team swears by Agile, while another is staunchly Waterfall. It's like watching cats and dogs try to agree on dinner plans. Different teams within an organization might adopt various methodologies, each believing in the superiority of their approach. This conviction can be so strong that it impedes the willingness to consider or integrate alternative, potentially more effective methods. When these methodologies are seen not just as different but as competing standards, it can fracture the cohesion of the broader engineering effort, preventing the synthesis of approaches that could lead to superior solutions.

Resource allocation often becomes a battleground where teams vie for the same budgetary, time, and human resources. Picture a medieval battlefield, but instead of swords, it's spreadsheets and project plans. When resources are seen as scarce, this competition can lead to conflict, where teams not only work to secure resources for themselves but also to deny them to others. This scenario fosters a climate of territoriality and protectionism, where teams are more likely to guard what they have rather than consider what could be optimally shared or redistributed according to project needs.

A desire for acknowledgment and the drive for visibility can also exacerbate inter-team conflicts. Teams or their leaders may become overly focused on ensuring their efforts are acknowledged, sometimes at the expense of collaborative success. This desire for the spotlight can lead to one-upmanship where the goal shifts from project success to individual or team recognition, fostering rivalry and reducing the incentive to work cooperatively towards common goals.

When projects encounter obstacles or fail, the dynamics of responsibility and accountability can deepen conflicts. It's like a high-stakes version of musical chairs, but no one wants to be left standing. Teams may shift blame to avoid repercussions, creating an environment where the focus is on avoiding fault rather than addressing underlying issues. This situation is detrimental not just to the resolution of the immediate problem but also to the overall culture within the organization, as it discourages openness and honesty in reviewing failures and impedes learning and development.

Unchecked inter-team conflicts, driven by differing methodologies, resource competition, a quest for recognition, and even personal jealousy, can profoundly affect an organization. These conflicts, if left unresolved, drain energy and resources and fundamentally alter the dynamics and potential of a company.

When teams are embroiled in disputes, the focus shifts from productive endeavors to maintaining territorial boundaries and managing internal strife. This redirection of focus results in significant time and resource waste. Energy that could otherwise be directed towards innovation and development. Such inefficiencies can slow down project timelines and increase costs as efforts are duplicated or redirected to manage or mitigate conflicts.

The constant stress and tension of ongoing conflicts can severely impact team morale. When team members focus more on internal disputes or protecting their status within the organization, job satisfaction can plummet. This often leads to increased turnover rates, as employees leave in search of healthier work environments. High turnover not only disrupts project continuity but also incurs additional costs related to recruiting and training new employees.

Jealousy and rivalry can lead teams to become protective of their ideas and innovations, choosing to hoard information rather than share it across the organization. This siloing of knowledge and creativity severely limits the organization's ability to innovate comprehensively. Instead of leveraging diverse perspectives and expertise to foster breakthrough innovations, the organization misses out on potential synergistic opportunities that could arise from more collaborative interactions.

Addressing these root causes of inter-team conflicts requires a concerted effort to foster a culture of openness, shared goals, and mutual respect. By recognizing and addressing these deep-rooted differences, organizations can create a more collaborative and productive environment that leverages the strengths of all teams.

Next time you find yourself in a heated debate over which project management tool is superior, remember: the goal isn't to win the argument, but to find a solution that brings everyone to the finish line together. Let's turn these medieval battles into modern-day collaborations, one team-building exercise at a time. And how would we do that? How do we navigate and resolve those conflicts?

Navigating and Resolving Conflicts

Alright, we've established that inter-team conflicts can make the workplace feel like a high-stakes drama series. But fear not! There's a way to turn this Game of Thrones into Friends. Here's how we navigate and resolve these conflicts with a healthy dose of humor and humanity.

First things first, communication is key. Imagine trying to build a Lego castle without talking to your fellow builders; chaos, right? Organizations need to foster an environment where open communication is genuinely encouraged and seen as the norm. Although many claim to do this, the reality is often different, as employees' input is frequently dismissed as arguing or complaining. We need to change that and encourage teams to share their goals, challenges, workflows, and successes transparently. Regular inter-team meetings that facilitate this type of exchange are crucial. And let's spice them up! These meetings shouldn't just be procedural but should aim to genuinely bridge understanding gaps and foster a spirit of cooperation and mutual support. When teams understand each other's challenges and workflows, it reduces misinterpretations and builds empathy. Think of it as a team-building exercise, but with fewer trust falls and more honest conversations.

Aligning all team efforts towards a unified set of organizational objectives is like getting everyone to paddle in the same direction. Otherwise, you're just going in circles. Each team should understand how their specific goals fit into the larger picture of the company's success. This alignment helps prevent conflicts that arise from teams pushing in different directions or competing for resources without regard to overall strategic goals. Leaders should regularly communicate these overarching goals and work with team leads to ensure that each team's objectives advance these broader targets. It's like making sure all the instruments in an orchestra are playing the same symphony.

Conflict is inevitable, but how it is managed can make the difference between a constructive outcome and a detrimental one. Establishing clear, effective, and fair conflict resolution mechanisms is key. Think of it as having a referee in a sports match. Someone neutral who can mediate and ensure fair play. This might include the use of mediation by neutral parties, providing a safe space where issues can be addressed without fear of reprisal. These mechanisms should be well understood by everyone and should be seen as a positive tool for improvement, not just a means to discipline or assign blame.

A powerful way to encourage collaboration over competition is to celebrate successes that result from joint efforts. Recognizing and rewarding teamwork, cross-team initiatives, and collaborative achievements reinforces the value of working together. Celebrations and rewards for collaborative successes should be public and meaningful, providing teams with a strong incentive to seek out and engage in cooperative ventures. Think of it like giving out gold stars, but these ones come with bonuses and public recognition.

Instead of a culture that focuses on blaming individuals or teams when things go wrong, cultivate an environment that views mistakes and conflicts as opportunities for growth. Encouragement should be given not only to success but also to constructive handling of failures. Leaders must model this behavior by how they handle project setbacks and inter-team disputes, focusing on what can be learned and how similar issues can be prevented in the future. After all, every failure is just a stepping stone to success, unless of course it's a catastrophic failure, in which case, maybe don't repeat that one.

Navigating conflicts within engineering teams requires a nuanced approach where leaders and engineers are equipped with strategies to handle disputes effectively, maintaining a balance between collaboration and assertiveness. Here's a strategic guide on when to pick your battles:

- **When to Ignore:** Not all conflicts warrant escalation. Sometimes, it's best to let minor disagreements slide. It's like choosing not to argue about whether pineapple belongs on pizza (it doesn't). Leaders and engineers should develop the discernment to recognize when a disagreement is minor and unlikely to impact the overall project or team dynamics significantly. This approach helps maintain a positive work atmosphere and conserves energy for more critical issues.
- **When to Play Along:** Compromise isn't just about making concessions; it's a strategic decision that can enhance teamwork and project integration. Leaders and engineers should identify opportunities where compromise facilitates better cooperation and integration across teams, without undermining essential project quality or objectives. By choosing this path in suitable situations, they can foster a collaborative environment and often achieve more sustainable and inclusive outcomes that benefit the entire project.
- **When to Stand Firm:** There are times when the stakes are high; be it the project's success, adherence to core values, or critical quality standards, where it becomes necessary to take a firm stand. Leaders and engineers need to be prepared to defend their positions assertively in such scenarios. This involves providing clear, rational justifications for their stances and effectively communicating

the potential consequences of not adhering to certain principles or standards. Standing firm in these situations is essential to maintain the integrity of the project and the values of the team.

By implementing these strategies, both leaders and engineers can more effectively navigate office politics, turning potential conflicts into opportunities for growth and innovation. The aim is to transform office politics from a hurdle into a catalyst for fostering a progressive, transparent, and highly collaborative work environment. This not only enhances project outcomes but also contributes to a more satisfying and productive workplace for everyone involved.

Conclusion: Cultivating a Collaborative Culture

Navigating the complex dance of inter-team dynamics within an organization is like trying to herd cats while juggling flaming torches. It demands a delicate balance between cooperative and assertive behaviors, a bit of humor, and a whole lot of patience. When organizations prioritize creating an environment that fosters open communication, mutual respect, and shared goals, potential conflicts can transform into opportunities for growth and innovation. Think of it as turning lemons into lemonade, but with a tech twist.

Creating a collaborative culture is akin to making a well-crafted stew: it requires the right ingredients, time, and attention. Leadership plays a crucial role in setting the tone for collaboration by modeling the behaviors they wish to see in their teams. Just as a good chef tastes their stew before serving it, leaders should actively encourage transparency, where sharing information and ideas is not just welcomed but expected. This openness allows for diverse perspectives to come to the fore, enriching the problem-solving process and leading to more innovative solutions.

Moreover, fostering mutual respect among team members is essential. Respecting each other's expertise, experiences, and viewpoints creates a safe space for collaboration. In such an environment, team members feel confident to voice their ideas and concerns without fear of ridicule or dismissal. This respect extends to recognizing and appreciating the contributions of all team members, ensuring that everyone feels their efforts are valued. Remember, a wise man once said, "Respect is like a smile; it costs nothing but means everything."

Shared goals are another cornerstone of a collaborative culture. When teams have a clear understanding of the common objectives and how their individual efforts contribute to these goals, it unites them in their pursuit. This alignment not only enhances motivation but also reduces the likelihood of conflicts arising from competing interests. Regular team meetings to review progress, address challenges, and celebrate successes can reinforce this sense of shared purpose. It's like making sure everyone is rowing in the same direction, otherwise, you're just going in circles.

Resolving inter-team conflicts requires proactive strategies. Organizations should establish clear conflict resolution protocols that emphasize dialogue and mediation. Encouraging teams to address conflicts early and directly helps prevent minor issues from escalating. Training in conflict resolution and communication skills can empower team members to handle disagreements constructively, turning potential discord into opportunities for deeper understanding and cooperation. Think of it as conflict alchemy; turning lead into gold.

It's important to recognize that competition between teams can be counterproductive. While healthy competition can drive performance, it should never come at the expense of collaboration. Organizations should focus on creating an atmosphere where teams view each other as allies rather than adversaries. This can be achieved by promoting inter-team projects, where success is defined by collective achievement rather than individual accolades. After all, "A rising tide lifts all boats."

Supporting one another towards innovation and common goals means recognizing that the success of one team contributes to the success of the entire organization. Facilitating knowledge sharing through cross-functional workshops, seminars, and collaborative platforms can enhance inter-team learning and synergy. This not only accelerates innovation but also builds a strong sense of community within the organization. It's like a potluck dinner, everyone brings something to the table, and everyone leaves full and happy.

In conclusion, cultivating a collaborative culture is not a one-time effort but an ongoing commitment. It requires consistent nurturing of open communication, mutual respect, and shared goals. By fostering an environment where collaboration is the norm and conflicts are resolved constructively, organizations can unlock the full potential of their teams. This approach ensures that every team member feels valued and motivated to contribute to the collective success, driving innovation and maintaining a competitive edge in the dynamic world of software engineering. So, let's roll up our sleeves, stir the pot, and make some magic happen!

Chapter 9

The Evolving Landscape of Software Engineering

BEYOND TECHNICAL SKILLS

Once upon a time, in a land not too far away, software engineers were seen as the mysterious wizards of the tech world. Armed with arcane knowledge of code, they toiled away in dimly lit rooms, casting spells of logic and syntax to summon working software from the ether. But oh, how times have changed!

As we dive into the ever-evolving world of software engineering, it's clear that the role of the software engineer has transformed dramatically. No longer are technical skills the sole metric of success in this field; soft skills and business acumen now play pivotal roles in shaping the careers of today's engineers. Software engineers are now like Swiss Army knives, packed with multiple tools to tackle an array of challenges beyond just writing code.

Historically, software engineers focused predominantly on writing code, debugging issues, and maintaining systems. They were like the dependable mechanics of the digital world, fixing what was broken and making sure everything ran smoothly. However, as the industry's needs have grown more complex, so have the responsibilities of these professionals. Engineers are increasingly expected to be versed in DevOps practices, merging development with operations to streamline and enhance both the creation and implementation phases of software development through continuous integration and continuous delivery (CI/CD). The rise of Agile methodologies has further shifted the focus towards rapid development cycles, requiring adaptability and close collaboration with stakeholders and team members. Additionally, the emphasis on user experience has expanded the engineer's role to include considerations of usability and experience in their design, beyond mere functionality.

Let's face it, being a software engineer today is like being part of an elite squad in a high-stakes mission, where every team member's skills and coordination are crucial. The importance of soft skills in the field of software engineering has grown significantly, paralleling the evolution of the engineer's role from a strictly technical expert to a versatile, multidisciplinary professional.

In today's fast-paced, Agile-driven environment, the ability to swiftly adapt, problem-solve, and collaborate across various domains is not just beneficial but essential. Once perhaps overlooked in the tech space, these skills are now crucial:

- **Communication**: No longer confined to monosyllabic grunts and the occasional meme, engineers must now engage not just with their immediate teams but also with a broader network of stakeholders, product managers, and clients. Effective communication ensures that project goals are understood and met, and that expectations are clearly set and managed. This skill is critical in avoiding misalignments that can lead to project delays and increased costs.

· **Teamwork and Collaboration**: Remember those group projects in school where one person did all the work? Yeah, that doesn't fly in the professional world. Engineering projects increasingly depend on cross-functional teams. The integration of diverse skill sets, perspectives, and expertise fuels innovation and drives the project forward. Engineers who can collaborate effectively contribute to a team's synergy and are instrumental in harnessing collective strengths to solve complex problems.

· **Problem-Solving and Adaptability**: Imagine being MacGyver, but instead of a Swiss Army knife, you have a keyboard and a caffeine addiction. Engineers are often confronted with novel challenges that require not only technical acumen but also creative thinking and an ability to pivot as circumstances change. This agility is especially important in Agile environments, where the shift from exhaustive pre-planning to iterative development necessitates continual learning and flexibility.

· **Leadership**: Senior engineers often find themselves in the role of the wise old sage, guiding projects and mentoring junior colleagues. These leaders shape the project's direction and make crucial decisions that affect the project's structural and operational integrity. Their ability to lead effectively can significantly impact the success of their team and the broader organization.

In summary, as software engineering continues to evolve, the blend of technical proficiency with strong soft skills becomes crucial. Engineers equipped with both sets of skills are better positioned to navigate complex project landscapes, lead effectively, and contribute to the innovation and success of their organizations.

The Leadership Role of Senior Engineers

In the realm of software engineering, senior engineers often embody the quintessence of leadership, transcending traditional managerial roles to become pivotal figures within their teams and projects. Their leadership is not just a byproduct of their seniority; it is a critical component of their role, enabling them to drive projects towards successful outcomes while fostering an environment of growth and innovation.

Senior engineers take on the mantle of leadership by guiding the strategic direction of projects. This involves not only planning and execution but also foreseeing potential challenges and opportunities that could impact the project's success. Their deep technical expertise allows them to make informed decisions about the architecture and technologies that will best serve the project in both the short and long term. By doing so, they ensure the project's structural and operational integrity, which are essential for scalability and sustainability.

Moreover, leadership for senior engineers involves mentoring and developing junior colleagues. This aspect of their role is crucial in building a resilient team. Through mentoring, senior engineers pass on valuable skills, insights, and professional standards to the next generation of engineers. They help junior team members understand complex technical concepts, encourage them to think critically about problems, and foster a culture of continuous learning and improvement. This mentorship not only enhances the team's overall capabilities but also ensures a legacy of quality and excellence.

Effective leadership by senior engineers also includes stakeholder management. They often act as the bridge between the technical team and non-technical stakeholders, including management, clients, and other departments. By effectively communicating technical details and project needs, they ensure that all parties are aligned, which is crucial for meeting project goals and expectations.

Ultimately, the leadership provided by senior engineers is indispensable for the health of the project and the organization. Their ability to lead effectively influences not just the success of the projects they oversee but also the broader organizational culture. It promotes a standard of excellence, drives innovation, and ensures that the company remains at the forefront of technological advancement. Senior engineers as leaders not only guide their projects to success but also shape the future direction of their organizations. So what are the implications for career development?

Implications for Career Development

In today's rapidly evolving tech landscape, continuous career development is not just beneficial; it's essential for engineers who aim to stay relevant and excel. As the role of the engineer expands beyond the confines of mere coding and system maintenance to encompass broader aspects of project and business management, the need for a diverse skill set becomes increasingly critical.

To thrive in modern engineering roles, engineers must commit to lifelong learning. This means consistently updating technical skills to keep pace with new programming languages, tools, and technologies. It also involves embracing practices like DevOps and Agile methodologies, which require a holistic understanding of the software development lifecycle beyond traditional coding tasks.

Equally important is the development of soft skills. Communication, teamwork, adaptability, and problem-solving are pivotal. Engineers must be able to articulate complex technical details to non-technical stakeholders clearly and concisely, ensuring alignment and facilitating project success. They must also navigate and adapt to the dynamic nature of tech projects where requirements, scopes, and team dynamics can shift rapidly.

Organizations can support their engineers by providing opportunities for cross-disciplinary training that bridges the gap between engineering and other areas of the business. This might include rotations in different departments, participation in leadership training programs, or involvement in customer-facing roles. Such experiences enhance engineers' understanding of the business implications of their work and foster a broader perspective that can lead to innovative solutions and improved decision-making.

Cultivating an environment that values and encourages the development of soft skills is also crucial. This can be achieved through team-building activities, collaborative projects, and a culture that values diverse viewpoints and inclusive decision-making. When engineers feel supported in developing these skills, they are more likely to engage fully, contribute to their fullest potential, and drive innovation within their teams.

Engineers should proactively seek out mentors and engage in networking within and beyond their organizations to learn from others' experiences and insights. Additionally, they should advocate for their career development needs, seeking out projects that challenge their current skill set and allow them to grow into well-rounded tech professionals.

In conclusion, the implications for career development in software engineering are profound. Engineers must continually adapt and evolve, not only to keep up with technological changes but also to anticipate and drive innovations. By embracing both technical and soft skills development, engineers can achieve career longevity and effectiveness, making them invaluable assets to their teams and companies.

So, fellow tech adventurers, as we navigate this ever-changing landscape, let's remember to equip ourselves with both the technical tools and the soft skills that will lead us to new heights. And if all else fails, remember the proverb: "The best way to predict the future is to create it." Let's go out there and create a future we're proud of!

Conclusion: A Holistic Approach to Engineering

Imagine software engineering as a grand orchestration, where every engineer is a maestro, wielding their keyboards like batons to create a symphony of code. The transformation in software engineering roles mirrors broader shifts in technology and business landscapes. In the evolving world of software engineering, the role of the engineer has expanded significantly beyond traditional boundaries. Today's successful engineer is not only a proficient coder but also an adept communicator, a strategic thinker, a collaborative team member, and often a leader.

Gone are the days when engineers could simply hide behind their monitors, shunning all human contact. The modern engineer must navigate not only the complexities of code but also the intricacies of team dynamics, client interactions, and project management. This holistic approach underscores the critical importance of integrating technical skills with soft skills, highlighting an era where such a blend is invaluable. Recognize the engineer as a pivotal figure in the strategic execution of business objectives, akin to a superhero who, instead of saving the world from villains, saves projects from catastrophic bugs and feature creep.

The rapid pace of technological advancement demands that engineers not only keep up with the latest developments but also anticipate future trends. This requires a continuous learning mindset and adaptability that goes beyond traditional engineering training. Picture an engineer as a lifelong student, perpetually enrolled in the university of technology, where the only constant is change. Engineers must now understand the broader business implications of their work, making decisions that balance technical excellence with practical business outcomes. It's like juggling flaming swords while riding a unicycle. It is challenging, but thrilling when done right!

Soft skills such as communication, teamwork, empathy, and leadership are becoming increasingly critical. Engineers must be able to effectively articulate complex ideas to stakeholders who may not share their technical background. This communication bridges the gap between technical solutions and business needs, ensuring that projects not only succeed technically but also deliver real business value. Think of it as translating geek into chic, making the intricate sound intriguing and essential to the uninitiated.

Today's engineers are often required to take on leadership roles, whether formally or informally. This involves mentoring junior colleagues, driving strategic project decisions, and sometimes challenging the status quo to ensure the long-term health of the engineering output. Leadership in engineering today means having a vision that extends beyond the code; to understand and influence how technology choices will affect the business now and in the future. It's like being a Jedi Knight, wielding the force of technology with wisdom and foresight to guide the galaxy (or at least the project) towards a prosperous future.

As we embrace this holistic approach, the distinction between 'engineer' and 'leader' becomes increasingly blurred. Engineers are expected to be at the forefront of innovation, advocating for technical excellence while also considering the larger business context. This dual focus makes them indispensable to the modern enterprise, not just as executors of tasks but as architects of the future. By fostering an environment that nurtures these diverse skills, organizations can leverage their engineering teams to drive not only technological advancement but also significant business growth. In essence, we're crafting a new breed of engineers who are part artist, part scientist, part diplomat, and entirely indispensable.

Chapter 10

Rethinking Middle Management

THE SHIFTING ROLE IN MODERN SOFT-WARE TEAMS

Transitioning from the evolving landscape of software engineering, where engineers have donned multiple hats to drive innovation, we now turn our attention to the intriguing realm of middle management redundancy. Yes, you heard it right! As engineers take on more responsibilities and AI advancements stride forward, the traditional role of middle management is up for a reevaluation.

In the rapidly evolving world of software engineering, the role of middle management is undergoing a critical transformation. Once deemed essential, the necessity of traditional middle management roles is being questioned as the competencies of technical professionals grow and as artificial intelligence tools become more sophisticated. This chapter explores the emerging trends that are redefining middle management and proposes new paradigms for their roles in software development teams.

Traditionally, middle managers in software development have been pivotal in bridging the gap between strategic directives from upper management and the operational execution by technical teams. They have handled project management, facilitated communication, and coordinated team efforts. However, the landscape is shifting. The evolving landscape of software teams increasingly underscores the diminishing role of traditional middle management as senior engineers and AI tools reshape team dynamics and organizational structures.

The role of senior engineers in the modern software team has expanded far beyond the technical realm of writing and debugging code. Today, these engineers are increasingly seen not just as team members, but as key players in project management and strategic decision-making. This shift is largely due to their deepening proficiencies in leadership, communication, and strategic planning, which enable them to directly manage projects and make critical decisions that were once the preserve of middle managers. By harnessing these enhanced capabilities, senior engineers are stepping into roles that require them to act as bridge-builders between the visionary goals of upper management and the practical, day-to-day activities of development teams.

This empowerment has significant implications for the structure of teams and the workflow within organizations. Senior engineers with a strong command of soft skills are now able to lead by example, fostering a culture of open communication and innovation. They can effectively translate high-level business strategies into actionable engineering goals, and by doing so, they reduce the layers of bureaucracy that can stifle innovation and responsiveness.

Complementing the rise of senior engineers are the advancements in AI and automation technologies. AI tools are now capable of performing a range of tasks traditionally managed by middle managers, such as resource scheduling, progress tracking, and even analyzing the complexities of project management to optimize timelines and team allocations. These technologies not only streamline operations but also introduce a level of precision and efficiency that human managers may find challenging to achieve consistently.

AI's ability to assist in these areas changes the expectations and functions of human managers, shifting their roles from overseeing mundane tasks to tackling more complex, strategic challenges that require human insight and creativity.

Imagine you're in a Zoom meeting, surrounded by the familiar faces of your colleagues, each ready to dive into the intricacies of release plans and sprint goals. You've got project updates, task allocations, and a sprinkle of light-hearted banter about who still hasn't fixed the coffee machine in the break room. Traditionally, after this meeting, a middle manager would dutifully take notes, summarize the discussion, assign action items, and distribute a comprehensive document to everyone involved. It's a task that, while essential, often felt like herding cats, meticulously documenting who said what, who promised to do what, and making sure nothing falls through the cracks.

And now the AI Companion enters the room. This nifty tool, with just a click of a button, listens attentively to the entire meeting. As the meeting concludes, it promptly generates a detailed summary, complete with action items, speaker attributions, and deadlines. The AI not only captures the essence of the conversation but also ensures that every decision and task is accurately documented, effectively doing the heavy lifting that once fell squarely on the shoulders of middle managers.

This technological marvel doesn't just stop at meeting notes. AI tools are now capable of performing a range of tasks traditionally managed by middle managers, such as resource scheduling, progress tracking, and even analyzing the complexities of project management to optimize timelines and team allocations. These technologies not only streamline operations but also introduce a level of precision and efficiency that human managers may find challenging to achieve consistently.

The Diminishing Need and The Evolving Role of Middle Managers

As the capabilities of both senior engineers and AI tools expand, organizations are prompted to evaluate the efficiency and necessity of maintaining traditional middle management layers. This shift is compelling companies to assess the true value and necessity of these intermediary roles.

Cost Efficiency and Organizational Agility: By reducing the layers of middle management, companies can achieve significant cost savings. These savings stem not only from decreased salary expenditures but also from the reduced complexity in organizational communications and decision-making processes. A leaner management structure enhances the organization's agility, enabling quicker adjustments to market conditions and technological advancements. This streamlined approach minimizes the bureaucratic delays that often stifle innovation and slow down project timelines, allowing for a swifter operational tempo and more effective deployment of resources.

Direct Communication and Enhanced Decision-Making: One of the most significant advantages of reducing middle management is the improvement in communication channels. With fewer intermediaries, senior engineers have direct lines to upper management and leadership, ensuring that strategic directives are not lost or diluted through multiple layers of translation. This direct communication fosters a clearer understanding of high-level business goals, which senior engineers can more effectively translate into technical objectives and actions.

This model not only enhances the clarity and speed of communication but also empowers senior engineers by placing them at the heart of decision-making processes. With a comprehensive understanding of both the technical and strategic facets of projects, these engineers can make informed decisions swiftly without the need for extensive consultations up and down the management chain.

Automation and AI in Management: The role of AI and automation in reducing the need for traditional middle management cannot be overstated. AI tools are increasingly capable of handling routine management tasks such as scheduling, resource allocation, and performance tracking. These tools enable senior engineers to focus on higher-value activities, such as innovation and strategic planning, rather than getting bogged down in administrative tasks.

Furthermore, AI-enhanced analytics tools can provide insights that were traditionally mediated by middle managers, such as project risk assessments and optimization of team workflows. This not only speeds up the decision-making process but also enhances its accuracy, as decisions are increasingly data-driven and less subject to human bias. With this shifting landscape the role of the middle manager must evolve as well.

The shifting landscape of technology demands a reevaluation of the role middle managers play in software development environments, especially those lacking technical expertise. As organizations recognize the importance of strategic leadership over routine oversight, the evolving role of middle managers can significantly enhance organizational efficiency and innovation.

Strategic Contributors: In the modern tech landscape, middle managers are ideally positioned to serve as strategic contributors rather than just overseeing day-to-day operations. Their deep understanding of the company's goals allows them to spearhead initiatives that align with long-term strategic objectives. This shift from a purely supervisory role to one of strategic significance requires them to understand both the technological aspects of projects and the broader business implications. As strategic contributors, they become essential in bridging the gap between the executive vision and operational execution, ensuring that projects not only align with but also advance business objectives.

Mentors and Coaches: Middle managers have a crucial role to play in talent development. By shifting their focus towards mentoring and coaching, they can cultivate a workforce that is versatile in both technical prowess and essential soft skills such as communication, teamwork, and problem-solving. This aspect of their role is particularly important in nurturing junior engineers and new hires, providing them with the guidance needed to navigate complex project landscapes and fostering a culture of continuous learning and improvement.

Change Agents: As technologies evolve and new methodologies like Agile and DevOps reshape the operational landscape, middle managers can act as change agents. They are uniquely positioned to facilitate the seamless integration of new technologies and workflows into existing systems. Their role involves not just the adoption of these technologies but also championing these changes throughout the organization. By leading such transitions, they help minimize resistance, promote understanding, and ensure that new practices are adopted effectively and efficiently.

In summary, as we transition into a new era of software engineering, the role of middle management is being redefined. By embracing these changes, organizations can enhance their efficiency, foster innovation, and create a more dynamic and agile work environment. It's a brave new world out there, and the middle managers who adapt will be the ones who thrive.

Conclusion: A New Vision for Management

In the swiftly changing landscape of software development, it's clear that the days of traditional middle management are numbered. Empowered senior engineers and sophisticated AI tools are stepping up to the plate, making many of the old-school middle management tasks seem as outdated as dial-up internet. This shift compels organizations to rethink their management structures, favoring a model where strategic, creative, and technical leadership is decentralized and distributed among highly skilled senior engineers.

Imagine a world where senior engineers, with their unmatched expertise, are directly shaping the future of their projects and teams, unhindered by layers of bureaucracy. AI tools take over the everyday tasks like scheduling, resource allocation, and routine decision-making, previously the domain of middle managers. This transformation not only enhances organizational agility and reduces overhead costs but also fosters an environment where innovation is systematically woven into the operational fabric of the company.

For middle managers, this rapid evolution might feel like the rug is being pulled out from under their feet. But fear not! There's still a crucial role for those willing to adapt. By transforming into strategic contributors, mentors, and change agents, middle managers can retain their relevance and vitality within their organizations. Embracing these new roles is essential for driving innovation, mentoring future leaders, and navigating the complex challenges of modern software development.

Just as the proverb goes, "The bamboo that bends is stronger than the oak that resists." Middle managers who embrace this evolution can not only survive but thrive, contributing significantly to their organizations' growth and success. In this brave new world, flexibility, adaptability, and a forward-thinking mindset are the keys to staying competitive and making a lasting impact.

Chapter 11

Unleashing Creativity: How Automation is Transforming Software Development

Building on the discussions from the previous chapters on the evolving role of software engineers and middle management, we now turn our attention to how automation is playing a transformative role in software engineering. As explored earlier, the traditional tasks of middle managers are being reshaped by technological advancements, shifting their roles from operational supervisors to strategic contributors and facilitators.

This chapter delves deeper into the world of automation, specifically Continuous Integration/Continuous Deployment (CI/CD) pipelines and automated testing, and its profound impact on the software development process. We'll explore how these tools not only enhance workflow efficiency but also empower engineers to focus on innovation and creativity by reducing their routine task load.

The Power of Automation in Development

Automation is profoundly reshaping software development, introducing efficiencies and capabilities that extend well beyond mere task automation. Its impact is felt across various stages of the development process, transforming how teams approach, execute, and deliver projects.

Automation tools streamline the development process, drastically reducing the time and effort required for many tasks. Continuous Integration/Continuous Deployment (CI/CD) pipelines are prime examples of this transformation. These pipelines automate the integration and deployment of code, which significantly cuts down on manual intervention and reduces wait times. This not only speeds up the development cycles but also allows teams to push updates more frequently and with greater confidence.

One of the most significant advantages of automation lies in its ability to enhance the quality of software through automated testing and reduce errors. Automated testing frameworks execute pre-designed test scripts on software applications, systematically identifying bugs at early stages of the development cycle. This proactive approach to bug catching improves the overall quality of the code and significantly diminishes the likelihood of critical errors making it to the production stages. By catching errors early, teams can avoid costly and time-consuming fixes later in the development process.

Automation ensures that every iteration of software builds and deployments is carried out with the same consistency and precision, which is crucial for maintaining the quality and reliability of the end products. This consistency is vital in environments where multiple deployments or updates are made regularly. Automation eliminates the variability introduced by human error and ensures that every deployment meets the same high standards. This reliability is essential not only for maintaining service quality but also for ensuring that all regulatory and compliance requirements are consistently met.

Through these mechanisms, automation not only optimizes the workflow but also empowers teams to focus on higher-level tasks and creative problem-solving, pushing the boundaries of what is possible in software development. This shift not only enhances the technical capabilities of a team but also contributes significantly to the strategic and competitive positioning of the entire organization.

Shifting Focus to Creativity

The advent of automation in software development has catalyzed a significant shift in how engineers allocate their time and mental resources. By taking over routine and repetitive tasks, automation tools enable engineers to focus on more complex and creatively demanding aspects of software projects.

With the burden of monotonous tasks lifted, developers are free to devote their energies to innovation and creative problem solving. This shift is not just about saving time; it's about enhancing the quality of work and the satisfaction engineers derive from their jobs. Freed from the tedium, developers can explore cutting-edge solutions, experiment with new technologies, and push the boundaries of what their software can achieve. This focus on innovation not only leads to more advanced and capable software solutions but also propels the industry forward by setting new standards and opening up new possibilities.

Furthermore, the automation of routine tasks enables senior developers to expand their roles beyond the technical realm into strategic planning and project management. These are areas that have traditionally been the purview of middle managers. However, with the technical insight and experience that senior developers bring, their involvement can lead to more informed and effective strategic decisions. This role expansion is crucial not only for the direct impact on projects but also for the professional growth of the developers themselves. It provides them with a broader perspective on the business and strategic side of operations, enhancing their career trajectories and contributing to the company's strategic goals.

By enabling engineers to engage more deeply in innovative problem solving and strategic planning, automation is not just transforming the nature of software development tasks; it's reshaping the very roles and career paths within the industry. This shift fosters a more dynamic, engaged, and creatively fulfilling work environment, which is essential for both retaining top talent and driving technological advancement.

As we embrace automation in software development, we open doors to unprecedented levels of creativity and innovation. The proverb, "Necessity is the mother of invention," aptly captures the essence of this transformation. By alleviating the necessity of routine tasks, automation allows the true inventiveness of engineers to flourish. This not only elevates the quality of software but also redefines the roles within development teams, empowering engineers to become leaders and innovators.

In this new era, the combination of human creativity and machine efficiency creates a powerful synergy that propels the industry forward. Organizations that harness this potential will find themselves at the forefront of technological advancement, driving both their success and the broader progress of the software engineering field.

Conclusion: Embracing the Future of Automation

As we continue to integrate sophisticated automation tools into our development processes, we witness a profound transformation in the roles and structures within software teams. This evolution is not merely about enhancing operational efficiency; it's about fundamentally altering the fabric of software development.

Automation liberates engineers from the monotonous and repetitive, allowing them to focus on areas where they can make a significant impact: innovation, strategic decision-making, and project leadership. This shift is redefining what it means to be an engineer in today's world. No longer confined to the boundaries of coding and technical oversight, engineers are emerging as pivotal figures in shaping the strategic direction of projects and the technological trajectory of their organizations.

This paradigm shift extends beyond mere productivity improvements; it fosters a culture where creativity and strategic insight are at the forefront. Engineers are now key players in driving innovations that can redefine market norms and set new benchmarks for technology development. By empowering engineers to utilize their technical skills in concert with strategic thought processes, organizations are not only enhancing their competitive edge but are also better positioned to adapt to rapid market changes and emerging technological challenges.

In embracing the future of automation, we are not just streamlining processes but are also paving the way for a more dynamic, responsive, and innovative software development landscape. This is not just a trend but a fundamental evolution in how software development is approached and managed, promising a future where technology and creativity converge to create exceptional outcomes.

As the saying goes, "Creativity is intelligence having fun." By unleashing creativity through automation, we are not just improving efficiency; we are creating an environment where intelligence and creativity can truly thrive, leading to innovations that were once unimaginable.

Chapter 12

Remote Work in Software Development

EMBRACING FLEXIBILITY FOR ENHANCED PRODUCTIVITY

So far in "Innovate or Stagnate," we've delved into the drivers of innovation, explored how interruptions and endless short meetings can sabotage an engineer's creativity, and mapped out the evolution of engineering roles and the future they hold. We've even taken a deep dive into the realm of management, proposing ways for managers to adapt or risk becoming relics of a long-gone era. We've offered abundant strategies for overcoming these hurdles and emphasized what both engineers and leadership need to do to keep the innovation engine running. Now, let's zoom in on the remote work revolution. Despite its challenges, the benefits far outweigh the obstacles, promising a brighter, more flexible future for the world of software development. Spoiler alert: your pajamas might just be your new work uniform!

As the software development industry continues to evolve, remote work has become an increasingly pivotal aspect of the modern workplace. And that is exactly what this chapter will delve into, the transformative impact of remote work in software engineering, where, unlike many traditional roles that necessitate a physical presence, software development thrives on the flexibility that remote working arrangements provide.

With over 14 years of experience working remotely, I have witnessed firsthand the substantial benefits it offers in terms of enhancing both productivity and creativity among engineers. However, despite these advantages, there exists a palpable hesitancy among some organizational leaders to fully embrace remote work. This reluctance often stems from underlying issues of trust and traditional management practices, which we will explore in depth in the following chapter. Here, we will dissect both the substantial benefits of remote work and the reasons behind some leaders' reluctance, setting the stage for a comprehensive discussion on fostering trust in remote teams.

The Benefits of Remote Work

The benefits of remote work, particularly within the field of software development, are significant and multifaceted, offering numerous advantages that often surpass the challenges it presents. Central to these benefits is the unparalleled flexibility that remote work introduces to software engineers, allowing them to optimize productivity and creativity in ways that traditional office settings do not permit.

Reduced Interruptions: As we have discussed in previous chapters, one of the most tangible benefits of remote work is the significant reduction in daily interruptions commonly experienced in traditional office environments. In an office, impromptu meetings and casual drop-bys can frequently disrupt an engineer's flow, leading to decreased efficiency and a fragmented workday. Remote work, on the other hand, empowers engineers to control their interactions and manage their schedules more effectively, ensuring that their deep work periods are protected.

Flexible Hours and Creative Freedom: The conventional 9-to-5 workday often clashes with the peak productivity periods of software engineers, whose creative impulses do not adhere to a strict schedule. Remote work liberates engineers from these confines, allowing them to work during hours when their creativity naturally peaks, whether that's early in the morning, late at night, or in sporadic bursts throughout the day. This flexibility not only boosts individual output but also enhances overall job satisfaction, as engineers can align their work schedules with personal and professional rhythms.

The analogy of engineers as "chefs of coding" aptly illustrates this point; just as chefs experiment with ingredients when inspiration strikes, engineers too benefit from being able to immediately implement innovative ideas as they arise, regardless of the time of day. This spontaneous and intuitive approach to problem-solving is crucial for innovation and can be stifled by rigid scheduling.

Custom Work Environments: Beyond timing, remote work allows engineers to create personalized work environments tailored to their specific preferences and needs. This customization can range from ergonomic setups that prevent physical strain to personalized ambient settings that enhance concentration and creativity. By designing their own workspaces, engineers can create environments that are not only comfortable but also conducive to long periods of focused work, thus maximizing productivity.

Emphasizing Results Over Rigidity: The shift towards remote work in software engineering highlights a broader move away from rigid, time-bound work structures towards results-oriented practices. In this model, the emphasis is on the quality and impact of the work produced rather than the hours logged. This approach aligns with the intrinsic motivations of engineers who, much like entrepreneurs, are driven by outcomes and the success of their projects. When organizations recognize and support this shift, they unlock the potential for true innovation, mirroring the commitment and drive seen in startup cultures where the focus is on thriving, not just surviving.

By embracing these benefits, organizations not only cater to the professional preferences of their engineering teams but also set the stage for enhanced productivity, greater job satisfaction, and a more innovative company culture.

The Evolution of Communication

The evolution of technology has significantly enhanced the capacity for remote communication, making it easier than ever for software teams to collaborate effectively across geographic boundaries. The rise of advanced communication tools and platforms has been a game-changer, ensuring that teams can stay connected and coordinated, irrespective of their physical locations.

Platforms like Zoom, Slack, Microsoft Teams, and others have become staples in the remote work toolkit, enabling real-time communication that closely mirrors the immediacy of in-person interactions. These tools support a range of functionalities from video conferencing and live chat to project management and document sharing, all designed to facilitate seamless collaboration.

With these technologies, meetings can be scheduled to accommodate different time zones, ensuring all team members can participate in key discussions without the need for physical presence. This flexibility is particularly beneficial for small, agile teams who can decide on optimal meeting times that respect each member's schedule and work preferences, enhancing participation and effectiveness.

The traditional notion that personal collaboration can only be achieved within the confines of an office is becoming increasingly outdated. Digital communication tools have proven their efficacy, enabling dynamic interaction that rivals, and sometimes exceeds, the levels of engagement found in physical settings. For instance, developers who work remotely often rely on platforms like Slack not just for casual communication but for substantial collaborative efforts. These tools provide structured ways to discuss projects, troubleshoot issues, and share updates, often more efficiently than the conventional method of gathering in a meeting room.

Moreover, the office environment is not necessarily conducive to productivity for everyone. Many individuals find themselves wearing headphones to block out office noise or to avoid interruptions from well-meaning colleagues. This suggests that the office, with its inherent distractions, might not be the optimal place for deep, focused work. In fact, the ability to control one's work environment is a key benefit of remote work, allowing employees to create a setting that truly supports their productivity.

Today, even when team members are located in the same office, there is a strong tendency to communicate via digital channels. This shift reflects a broader change in workplace dynamics, where digital fluency is becoming more crucial than physical proximity. By utilizing digital tools, team members can maintain continuous connectivity, share instant updates, and access shared resources without the need to physically gather. This not only maintains efficiency but also empowers team members to interact on their terms, which can lead to more thoughtful and productive exchanges.

By embracing the potential of modern communication technologies, organizations can dismantle the traditional barriers imposed by physical office spaces. This not only supports a more flexible and inclusive working environment but also aligns with contemporary work practices where digital proficiency and flexibility are at a premium. In doing so, companies not only accommodate the changing preferences of their workforce but also position themselves as forward-thinking, adaptable entities in the evolving landscape of work.

In the realm of remote work, it's crucial to focus on results rather than obsessing over how many hours an engineer sits at their desk. After all, it's the quality of the work that matters, not how often someone jostles their mouse to look busy. As the saying goes, "You don't judge a tree by its leaves, but by the fruit it bears." Let's be results-focused, celebrating the innovations and solutions our engineers create, rather than micromanaging their every move. Remember, great things can happen even if those great minds are working in their pajamas!

Navigating the Challenges

While remote work offers numerous advantages for software engineers, it also introduces several challenges that can affect both individual well-being and team dynamics. Addressing these challenges is crucial for maintaining a healthy, productive remote work environment.

Communication Hurdles: Effective communication is the cornerstone of remote work success. In the absence of face-to-face interactions, misunderstandings can occur more frequently, potentially leading to project delays and decreased morale. Remote teams must emphasize clear, concise, and frequent communication. Employing comprehensive communication tools and establishing regular check-ins can help mitigate these risks, ensuring that every team member remains aligned with project goals and fully aware of their responsibilities.

Isolation and Loneliness: While some individuals thrive in a solitary work environment, others might struggle with the lack of social interaction that an office provides. This can lead to feelings of isolation or loneliness, which might diminish motivation and affect mental health. To address this, companies should foster a virtual community, encouraging social interactions through digital hangouts or casual meet-ups and ensuring that employees feel connected and supported.

Overworking and Work-Life Balance: One of the paradoxical effects of remote work is the tendency to work longer hours. The blurring lines between home and work can make it difficult for individuals to 'switch off' at the end of the day, potentially leading to burnout. Organizations can help prevent this by promoting a culture that values work-life balance. Encouraging employees to set and adhere to specific work hours, recognizing and respecting boundaries, and discouraging after-hours communication unless absolutely necessary are all effective strategies.

Overcoming these challenges requires proactive strategies and a commitment to creating a supportive remote work culture. Organizations can implement structured daily routines, invest in team-building activities, and use project management tools that keep everyone on track without feeling overwhelmed. Additionally, providing mental health resources and encouraging regular breaks can enhance productivity and safeguard employees' well-being.

In summary, while remote work does present certain obstacles, with the right tools and approaches, these challenges can be effectively managed. By fostering open communication, supporting social interactions, and promoting a healthy work-life balance, companies can harness the full potential of remote work, allowing their engineers not just to succeed but to thrive in a flexible work environment. So how do we overcome those and how do we ensure we thrive working remotely?

Best Practices for Thriving Remotely

To maximize the benefits and to harness the full potential of remote work, adopting best practices that facilitate productivity, collaboration, and well-being is essential. These practices help in recreating the benefits of physical office spaces while leveraging the unique advantages of remote work.

Consistent Communication: Consistent communication is vital to keep remote teams connected and focused. Regular check-ins, both formal and informal, are crucial for maintaining alignment on project goals and timelines. They also serve to foster relationships among team members, ensuring that everyone feels part of the team and is clear on their roles and responsibilities. These check-ins should include a mix of structured meetings for project updates and casual interactions that allow team members to connect on a personal level.

Leveraging Technology: Leveraging technology is at the heart of successful remote work. Tools like Slack for instant messaging, Zoom for video conferencing, and JIRA for project management are indispensable in creating an efficient remote work environment. These tools help in replicating the immediacy of office interactions, making communication seamless and ensuring that collaboration is as effective remotely as it would be in person.

Establishing Boundaries: One of the most significant challenges of remote work is the blurring of lines between personal and professional life. It is crucial to establish and respect clear boundaries. Employees should be encouraged to develop routines that clearly demarcate working hours from personal time. Organizations can support this by setting expectations for availability and respecting employees' time outside of those hours, helping to prevent burnout and maintain a healthy work-life balance.

Creating a Sense of Community: Creating a sense of community is key to mitigating the isolation that can come with remote work. Organizing virtual social events such as coffee breaks, lunch meetups, or team-building activities can help build connections and bolster team morale. These activities provide informal settings for team members to interact and bond, which is crucial for nurturing a cooperative and supportive work culture.

By implementing these best practices, companies can create a remote work environment that not only maintains productivity and efficiency but also enhances employee satisfaction and fosters a strong, cohesive team dynamic. This proactive approach to remote work ensures that all team members feel valued and integrated, despite the physical distances.

Conclusion: The Strategic Advantage of Remote Work

The shift towards remote work has proven itself to be more than a mere response to external circumstances; it is a strategic evolution that recognizes the changing dynamics of the workplace, particularly in the field of software development. Allowing engineers the flexibility to work remotely not only caters to their preferences for less structured environments but also taps into their peak hours of creativity and productivity, which do not always align with the traditional 9-to-5 schedule.

Organizations that adopt remote work demonstrate a progressive attitude towards workplace flexibility, which is a significant factor in retaining top talent. Software engineers often seek employers who trust them to perform without constant oversight and value the results they deliver over their physical presence in an office. By respecting these preferences, companies not only increase job satisfaction but also foster a sense of loyalty and commitment among their staff.

The autonomy associated with remote work allows engineers to manage their schedules in ways that maximize their productivity. Without the frequent interruptions of a traditional office environment, engineers can focus more intensely, leading to higher quality outputs and faster project turnaround times. This level of efficiency is crucial in a field where innovation and speed are often key determinants of market success.

For organizations, the benefits are manifold. Remote work reduces the need for extensive physical office space, which can translate into significant cost savings. More importantly, by facilitating a happier and more productive workforce, companies see a direct positive impact on their bottom line. Projects are completed more efficiently, innovation flourishes, and the company becomes more attractive to prospective employees.

In conclusion, as the technology sector continues to lead the way in workplace modernization, the integration of remote work into operational models is not just beneficial; it's imperative. Companies that embrace this flexibility will find themselves at the forefront of industry advancements, capable of attracting and retaining the best talent while driving significant innovation. This full-circle benefit enriches both the individuals and the organization, proving that the future of work lies in flexibility and strategic adaptation. As the saying goes, "The early bird catches the worm," but in the world of remote work, it's more like, "The flexible bird builds the best nest."

Chapter 13

Trust at the Core: Navigating Ethics and Privacy in the Digital Age

As the digital landscape continues to transform at an unprecedented rate, particularly with the rise of remote work, trust has become the cornerstone of modern organizational dynamics and technology ethics. In this chapter I am trying to aim to unpack the crucial role of trust within the context of today's tech-driven world. It addresses how trust influences not just the operational aspects of businesses, such as employee engagement and productivity, but also casts a wide net over critical ethical issues including privacy, data protection, and the moral obligations of corporations towards their stakeholders.

The trust dynamic in the digital age extends beyond traditional boundaries, challenging companies to foster environments where trust is not just an expected standard but a foundational business strategy. This becomes especially relevant as the reliance on digital platforms increases, both for internal operations and external interactions. Here, trust determines the quality of relationships among remote teams, the security of data handled by businesses, and the company's overall reputation in the marketplace.

Moreover, the chapter will discuss the delicate balance between leveraging advanced surveillance technologies intended to enhance productivity and the potential ethical pitfalls that such monitoring systems may entail. These systems, while designed to track efficiency, often inadvertently contribute to a culture of suspicion that can undermine trust and morale.

By exploring the implications of these developments, I am hoping that this chapter will provide insights into how businesses can navigate the complex terrain of ethics and privacy without compromising on the very trust that binds their teams and customers. It will argue that in an era where personal data has become a currency and personal space a commodity, the onus lies on organizations to build robust frameworks of trust that support innovation and integrity alike.

The evolving responsibilities of companies in safeguarding this trust reflect broader societal and ethical considerations that today's leaders must adeptly manage. The aim is to cultivate a discourse that promotes a deeper understanding of trust as a dynamic and potent facet of modern business practices and technological development, thereby fostering a sustainable and ethically conscious business environment.

The Ethical Dilemma of Employee Surveillance

In the modern workplace, particularly in remote settings, the use of surveillance software to monitor employees introduces profound ethical challenges that resonate across all levels of an organization. These tools, ranging from keystroke logging to continuous screen monitoring, are often justified under the guise of enhancing productivity and accountability. However, the implications of such surveillance extend far beyond the mere tracking of employee activities, ushering in a host of ethical concerns that can undermine the very fabric of trust and privacy within a company.

Erosion of Trust and Morale: The deployment of surveillance software often sends a clear message to employees: "You are not trusted." This sentiment can profoundly impact workplace morale and employee loyalty. The psychological burden of being constantly watched can induce stress and anxiety, conditions not conducive to creativity or productivity. When employees feel distrusted, their attachment to the organization weakens, and their motivation to exceed expectations diminishes. It begs the question; if trust is not extended to employees, why were they hired in the first place? Why did you hire me if you do not trust me? Trust and respect are fundamental in any relationship.

Invasion of Privacy: The pervasive nature of surveillance in the workplace can transform it into a panopticon where employees feel their every action is being monitored. This can lead to a significant invasion of privacy, blurring the lines between professional and personal life, especially in remote work scenarios where professional boundaries are already complex to navigate. The discomfort of being under constant observation restricts open communication and can stifle the natural flow of creativity and innovation, which are vital to the developmental processes in technology and software fields.

Impact on Innovation: In a field driven by innovative thinking and creative solutions, a monitored environment can deter employees from taking the necessary risks that fuel innovation. The fear of being watched and judged can discourage employees from experimenting with new, untested solutions, ultimately stifling growth and innovation within the organization. The very tools intended to boost productivity may instead curb the intellectual freedom required for genuine innovation.

These ethical dilemmas highlight the need for a balanced approach to employee monitoring, one that respects personal boundaries and fosters an environment of trust rather than surveillance. As we delve deeper into the impacts of these practices, it becomes increasingly clear that the ethical management of surveillance tools is not just a matter of policy but of upholding the core values of respect and dignity within the workplace.

Data Protection and User Privacy

Let's talk about data protection and user privacy. The importance of data protection and user privacy in the digital realm becomes increasingly paramount, not just as a functional necessity but as a core ethical standard in software development. As technologies evolve and the volume of personal data managed by software increases, organizations bear a significant responsibility to uphold the trust users place in them. This responsibility encompasses several key practices:

In an era where data breaches can lead to substantial financial and reputational damage, the protection of sensitive information is critical. Organizations must implement robust security measures to safeguard personal data against unauthorized access, theft, or leakage. This involves not only utilizing advanced encryption and security protocols but also regularly updating and testing these systems to address new vulnerabilities as they arise.

Transparency is the cornerstone of building trust with users. Companies need to be clear and upfront about how they collect, use, and store user data. This transparency not only helps in building user trust but also ensures compliance with increasingly stringent global data protection regulations. It is clear that accessible privacy policies and regular communication about data use can empower users, giving them control over their information.

Ensuring that users give informed consent regarding the collection and use of their data is not just a legal requirement; it's an ethical obligation. Users should be fully informed about what data is being collected, why it is being collected, how it will be used, and with whom it may be shared. This process involves providing users with straightforward options to either opt-in or opt-out of data collection schemes, emphasizing the voluntary nature of their participation.

Beyond the mechanical aspects of data security and user consent, ethical data management involves considering the user's rights and dignity at every step of the design and development process. This approach sees data protection as a design priority, not an afterthought, integrating privacy considerations into the product from the ground up.

These practices underscore the vital role that data protection and user privacy play in the integrity and success of software development projects. By adhering to these principles, organizations not only comply with legal standards but also enhance their reputational standing, fostering a more ethical and user-centric approach to technology development.

Social Impact of Technological Decisions

So we have discussed employee trust, user trust through transparency and data protection, and now let's talk about the social impact of technological decisions. The decisions made by technology leaders echo far beyond the confines of their immediate business outcomes, influencing wider societal landscapes. The responsibility to consider and address the broader social impacts of their technological choices is paramount. This encompasses several crucial aspects:

Digital Inclusion: Digital inclusion is very important. In a world increasingly governed by digital interactions, ensuring that technology is accessible to everyone is crucial. This means creating solutions that cater to diverse populations, including those with disabilities, those from varied socio-economic backgrounds, and those living in remote or underserved regions. By promoting digital inclusion, technology leaders can help bridge the digital divide, making it possible for more individuals to access information, services, and opportunities that are otherwise out of reach. Efforts here include developing products with universal design principles in mind and creating more affordable technology options.

Socio-Economic Equality: Technology has the power to either mitigate or exacerbate existing inequalities. Leaders must actively work to ensure that their technological innovations contribute positively to socio-economic equality. This involves considering how new technologies can provide opportunities for education, employment, and upward mobility to underserved communities, rather than creating greater barriers to access.

Environmental Sustainability: The environmental impact of technological advancements, particularly decisions regarding the location and operation of data centers, which consume vast amounts of energy, is significant. Leaders must prioritize sustainability, opting for renewable energy sources and striving for energy-efficient operations to minimize the carbon footprint of their technological infrastructures.

Ethical AI and Automation: The use of artificial intelligence in decision-making processes is increasingly common but comes with significant ethical considerations. Technology leaders must ensure that AI systems are designed and deployed responsibly, with mechanisms in place to prevent biases and ensure fairness and transparency. This also involves considering the long-term societal impacts of automation and AI on employment and personal privacy.

Community Engagement: Technology should not be developed in isolation from the communities it serves. Engaging with local communities to understand their needs and how technology can serve them better is essential. This engagement can inform more empathetic and effective technological solutions that resonate with and genuinely benefit users.

The overarching impact of technological decisions on societal well-being must be a guiding factor in the strategic planning of tech companies. This means looking beyond immediate business needs to how technology affects societal norms, individual behaviors, and the overall quality of life.

By addressing these aspects, technology leaders can ensure that their decisions contribute positively to society, fostering a technology landscape that is ethical, inclusive, and forward-thinking. This holistic approach is not only ethically sound but also aligns with a sustainable business model that values long-term societal impact alongside profitability.

Best Practices for
Ethical Decision-Making

Creating an ethical framework in technology management is essential not just for compliance but for fostering a culture of trust and safety that encourages innovation and stability. This framework must center around trust between all organizational members, from those in leadership positions to every employee without decision-making power.

Transparency: Transparency is the cornerstone of trust. Organizations must clearly articulate their policies on surveillance, data usage, and ethical conduct. This transparency helps to demystify the organization's operations for its employees and stakeholders, fostering trust and making it clear that the organization values integrity and openness. Clear policies ensure that every member of the organization understands their rights and the expectations placed upon them, reducing fears about overreach or misuse of authority.

Engagement: Engagement with all stakeholders, particularly employees, is crucial in building a supportive and ethical organizational culture. By involving employees in the creation and revision of policies, organizations can ensure that these policies are not only fair but also have the buy-in of those they affect most directly. This involvement helps to dissolve the barriers typically set by hierarchical structures, emphasizing that everyone, regardless of their role or authority level, has a valuable perspective that can contribute to the organization's ethical stance.

Security and Privacy: Prioritizing security and privacy is non-negotiable in the digital age. Rigorous security measures protect the integrity and confidentiality of data, which in turn protects the organization and its users from potential harm. This commitment must be more than nominal; it should include ongoing assessments and updates to security protocols to handle emerging threats. Demonstrating a commitment to robust security practices reassures all stakeholders that the organization is serious about its ethical responsibilities.

Employee Well-Being: Beyond policies and engagement, creating an environment where employees feel safe and trusted is essential for fostering innovation. When employees are assured that they are valued members of the organization and that their employment is stable, they are more likely to invest fully in their roles and innovate without fear. This security encourages risk-taking and creative problem-solving, which are critical for technological advancement and competitive advantage.

Practical Ethics: Finally, it is vital that ethical declarations are matched by practice. This includes training for all employees on ethical practices, regular audits of ethical compliance, and a clear channel for reporting unethical behavior without fear of retribution. Encouraging an open dialogue about ethics, and making it clear that ethical behavior is everyone's responsibility, reinforces the importance of these values.

By embedding these practices into the fabric of their operations, organizations not only protect themselves and their users but also build a foundation of trust that permeates every interaction within the workplace. This trust is crucial for long-term success and is a powerful driver of sustainable innovation.

In our organization, we take trust with our users very seriously. We go to great lengths to protect user data, implementing robust security measures and ensuring complete transparency in our processes. We want our users and customers to trust us implicitly because we understand that their confidence is crucial to our success. This commitment to trust is unwavering, driven by legal mandates and the financial transactions that sustain our business.

Yet, paradoxically, we often struggle to extend the same level of trust to our employees. Is it because data protection is legally mandated? Because our users are paying customers, whereas employees are seen as replaceable? The hesitancy to trust our employees manifests in remote work setups and the pervasive use of surveillance tools. It's ironic that we prioritize trust in our external relationships but hesitate internally, forgetting that a trusted, empowered workforce is equally vital to our success. If we can protect user data with such rigor, surely we can trust the people who help build and maintain these systems. After all, happy employees make for happy customers.

Retiring "It's Just Business": Humanizing Workplace Interactions

In the context of ethical decision-making and trust in the workplace, the often-used phrase "it's just business" warrants scrutiny and reconsideration. Traditionally employed to justify tough decisions or impersonal actions within a corporate environment, this phrase can inadvertently dehumanize workplace interactions and mask the essential human element inherent in every business transaction.

The expression "it's just business" is frequently used to depersonalize actions that might otherwise be seen as harsh or unfair. This can range from layoffs and harsh managerial decisions to invasive monitoring practices. While it's intended to separate personal feelings from business operations, the reality is that these decisions deeply affect the lives of individuals. They stir concerns about security, fairness, and respect; fundamental aspects that contribute to a trusting and ethical workplace.

Using "it's just business" to justify decisions that impact employees can lead to a breakdown in trust. Employees might feel that their well-being is secondary to profit or efficiency gains, leading to diminished loyalty and a workplace where individuals feel undervalued or disposable. This atmosphere can stifle open communication and innovation, as employees may be less inclined to contribute beyond the minimum required or to engage in creative problem-solving.

To foster a truly ethical and collaborative environment, organizations must move away from viewing decisions as purely business transactions and instead recognize the human impact of their choices. First and foremost, this involves empathy in leadership, then to build genuine relationships and of course to retire harmful phrases.

Leaders should strive to understand and consider the personal impacts of their decisions. Empathy should be a core leadership skill, guiding interactions and decisions to ensure they are made with consideration for the people involved.

Encouraging managers and leaders to build relationships based on mutual respect and understanding can help dismantle the impersonal nature often associated with business transactions. These relationships should be nurtured through regular, open communication and a genuine interest in the well-being of all employees.

Actively discouraging the use of "it's just business" and similar phrases can help shift the corporate culture towards one that values individual contributions and acknowledges the personal investment employees make in their work.

In modern business practices, particularly in fields driven by innovation such as technology, the success of an organization is increasingly dependent on the creativity, engagement, and well-being of its workforce. Recognizing that business is inherently personal and that each decision impacts real people with emotions and personal lives is crucial. By retiring the phrase "it's just business" and embracing a more humane approach to business interactions, organizations can foster a more ethical, trusting, and productive workplace.

Trust is not just an abstract ideal but a tangible force that shapes the success and sustainability of modern organizations. In the digital age, where technology and human interaction intersect more than ever, fostering trust is crucial. By prioritizing ethical practices, transparent communication, and genuine empathy, organizations can build environments where innovation thrives, employees feel valued, and long-term success is achieved.

As we navigate the complexities of the digital landscape, let us remember that "trust is the glue of life." It is the foundational principle that holds all relationships, whether personal or professional, together. By embracing trust as a core value, we can create workplaces that are not only more productive but also more humane, where the true potential of every individual and team can be realized.

Conclusion: Building a Culture of Trust

As we wrap up this chapter on trust and ethics within the technology sector, it's clear that fostering trust goes way beyond just ticking the boxes of legal compliance. It's about weaving ethical considerations into the very fabric of an organization's culture. We must remember that trust is not just another checkbox; it's a way of life that should influence every decision and interaction within and outside the organization.

Organizations that rely heavily on surveillance often send a message of fundamental mistrust. This approach can sink morale, choke creativity, and corrode the mutual respect needed for a productive work environment. Instead of playing Big Brother, we should be focusing on empowering our employees. Remember, "Trust is the glue of life. It's the most essential ingredient in effective communication. It's the foundational principle that holds all relationships" (Stephen Covey). By empowering employees, we're likely to see genuine and sustainable productivity gains.

The Pillars of a Trust-Based Culture

1. **Transparency:** When we're open about operations and decision-making, it builds trust. If employees understand the 'why' behind decisions, they are more likely to support them, even if they're affected by them. Think of it as "laying your cards on the table"; everyone knows the game and the stakes.
2. **Respect for Privacy:** Just as user privacy is paramount, so too is employee privacy. A workspace, virtual or physical,

that respects personal boundaries fosters a healthier, more innovative environment. As the saying goes, "Respect begets respect."

3. **Empowerment**: Providing employees with the tools, authority, and trust to make decisions encourages a more dynamic and responsive organization. This means recognizing their capabilities and allowing them to exercise their judgment. "Give a man a fish, and you feed him for a day. Teach a man to fish, and you feed him for a lifetime."

Beyond the internal benefits, ethical practices in technology contribute to the greater good. Companies that prioritize ethical considerations help set standards for privacy, inclusion, and fairness, influencing industry-wide practices and societal norms.

Finally, our conversation about trust and ethics is not limited to individual organizations. It's part of a larger dialogue that includes regulators, consumers, and the broader community. Engaging with these stakeholders helps refine ethical practices and ensures they are robust and relevant. "It takes a village," after all.

As we move forward, understanding and navigating the complexities of trust and ethics in technology will remain crucial. I encourage you to reflect on these themes within your own organizations. How do you balance productivity with privacy? What steps do you take to ensure your practices are ethical? Engaging in this ongoing dialogue will not only enhance your operations but also contribute positively to the larger community we all belong to.

Let's remember that trust, like a tree, takes years to grow but can be destroyed in a moment. So let's nurture it carefully.

Chapter 14

Global Insights: How Cultural Contexts Shape Software Engineering Practices

Having explored the critical role of trust in our previous chapter, it's equally important to understand how different cultures shape practices in the realm of software engineering. In the vast and ever-evolving field of software development, the subtle yet profound impact of cultural contexts on work practices cannot be overstated.

With a career spanning across the USA, Canada, Europe, and India, I have gained invaluable insights into how diverse cultural backgrounds influence software development. These experiences highlight that while software engineering is inherently technical, the human aspect, shaped by cultural norms and values of course, plays a critical role in the execution and outcome of software projects. And we must understand that.

This chapter delves deep into the myriad ways cultural nuances shape software engineering, affecting everything from team dynamics to problem-solving techniques, from decision-making processes to innovation paths. By exploring a variety of cultural settings, we uncover how local customs, business practices, and societal values not only dictate the 'how' of software engineering but also often determine its success or failure.

Through this exploration, we aim to broaden our understanding of how embracing cultural diversity can lead to more innovative solutions and a more inclusive approach to software development. This chapter not only highlights the opportunities that cultural diversity brings to software engineering but also addresses the challenges that arise in a globalized market, providing a holistic view of the interplay between culture and technology.

Diverse Practices, Diverse Innovations

We all know and understand that software engineering is in the global arena, and we must also understand that the influence of local demands and cultural expectations significantly shapes how development processes are adopted and adapted. This variety in practice does not merely reflect regional differences but actively contributes to a rich tapestry of innovations that enhance the field:

- **Agile in the West**: In North America and parts of Europe, Agile methodologies have become synonymous with software development, underscoring a cultural emphasis on flexibility, iterative learning, and extensive collaboration. This approach aligns with Western values that prioritize individualism, innovation, and direct communication, fostering environments that encourage rapid adaptation to change and continuous improvement.

· **Systematic Approaches in Europe**: Many European nations draw upon their deep historical roots in structured thought, and this goes all the way from Roman legal systems to the Industrial Revolution, to shape their approaches to software engineering. The result is a highly systematic framework that meticulously plans and documents each phase of the software development process. This meticulousness ensures high reliability and scalability of software solutions, catering to Europe's preference for durability and long-term value over quick fixes.

· **Frugal Innovation in India**: India's unique contribution to software engineering, often termed 'Jugaad,' revolves around an improvisational style of innovation that makes a virtue of necessity. This approach is not about making do but making things possible within the constraints of cost and resources. It has propelled India to the forefront of developing flexible and cost-effective solutions that are not only robust but also scalable across diverse global markets, proving particularly advantageous in sectors where resource constraints are a significant consideration.

These distinct practices underscore a broader principle: local cultural contexts deeply influence not only the 'how' of software engineering but also the 'what' and 'why.' These diverse methodologies enrich the global software landscape, providing a competitive edge and driving innovation that respects and reflects the diverse needs and constraints of various markets.

For instance, consider the approach to mobile app development. In the United States, the focus might be on creating feature-rich applications with a strong emphasis on user experience and design, driven by a culture that values innovation and consumer satisfaction. American developers often leverage the latest technologies and frameworks to build cutting-edge apps that offer seamless user interactions and robust functionality.

In contrast, in countries like India, where resource constraints and a diverse user base present unique challenges, developers often prioritize efficiency and accessibility. This has led to the rise of 'frugal innovation,' where engineers create solutions that deliver maximum functionality with minimal resources. For example, the development of lightweight mobile applications that consume less data and work efficiently on lower-end devices has become a hallmark of Indian software engineering. This approach ensures that technology is accessible to a broader audience, reflecting the local market's needs and constraints.

Meanwhile, in Europe, the emphasis on data privacy and stringent regulatory standards like GDPR influences software development practices. European developers often focus on creating secure and compliant applications, ensuring that user data is protected and privacy regulations are adhered to. This cultural context drives innovation in areas such as data encryption, user consent mechanisms, and transparent data handling practices.

These examples highlight how diverse practices can drive diverse innovations. By integrating these varied approaches, global software companies can create more comprehensive and adaptable solutions. An app developed with the user-centric design principles from the US, the efficiency and accessibility focus from India, and the privacy and security standards from Europe could potentially offer a superior product that meets the needs of a global audience.

Such cross-cultural integration not only enriches the software development process but also enhances the product's relevance and appeal across different markets. It underscores the importance of embracing cultural diversity in engineering practices to drive innovation and maintain a competitive edge in the global market.

Cultural Challenges to Innovation

Expanding on the cultural challenges to innovation, it becomes evident that while diversity can drive creativity and innovation, it also brings complexities that can slow or even halt progress in software engineering:

- **Bureaucracy and Red Tape**: In many European and Asian countries, a dense layer of bureaucracy often surrounds technological and business processes. These systems, steeped in traditional and sometimes outdated practices, can impose rigid procedural requirements that are not only time-consuming but also discouraging for innovators. This bureaucratic inertia can significantly delay or deter the implementation of new technologies and agile methodologies, creating barriers that are often hard to overcome. The need for numerous approvals and adherence to strict guidelines can suppress spontaneity in innovation and discourage the agile, experimental approaches necessary for breakthroughs in technology.
- **Risk Aversion**: A profound cultural aversion to risk is another significant impediment to innovation observed across various global regions. In societies where maintaining the status quo is preferred and the potential consequences of failure are heavily stigmatized, there is often a reluctance to invest in unproven technologies or innovative processes. This conservative approach can inhibit companies from pioneering new markets or adopting cutting-edge technologies, potentially causing them to miss out on substantial opportunities. The cautious pace

of technology adoption ensures stability and continuity but often at the cost of slowing innovation and reducing competitive edge in rapidly evolving tech landscapes.

These cultural challenges underscore the need for a balanced approach that encourages innovation while managing risks prudently. Addressing these issues requires not just changes at the organizational level but also a broader cultural shift towards a more dynamic and adaptive view of technological advancement and business practices.

For example, let's consider a software company in Germany, renowned for its meticulous attention to detail and structured processes. While these characteristics ensure high-quality and reliable software, they can also lead to extensive red tape and bureaucratic hurdles. I recall a project where we were developing a new enterprise application for a German customer, and I was on that project for a few years. The approval process for even minor changes involved multiple layers of management and extensive documentation. This rigorous approach, while thorough, significantly slowed down our development cycle and dampened the team's enthusiasm for exploring innovative solutions.

To address this, we introduced a more flexible project management framework that blended the best of both worlds: maintaining the German precision in quality while adopting Agile practices to enhance responsiveness and adaptability. We created cross-functional teams empowered to make decisions quickly, reducing the layers of approval needed. This approach required a cultural shift within the organization, encouraging managers to trust their teams and embrace a more iterative and experimental mindset.

The results were remarkable. Not only did the development speed improve, but the team also felt more motivated and engaged, knowing their innovative ideas could be implemented without excessive delays. This experience highlighted the importance of balancing meticulous planning with agility, showing that with the right cultural shift, it's possible to overcome the challenges posed by traditional bureaucratic systems.

By fostering an environment that values both structure and flexibility, organizations can better manage risks while still encouraging innovation. This balanced approach helps create a dynamic and adaptive business culture that is well-equipped to navigate the complexities of modern technology landscapes.

Another example is when I was on a project in India, tasked with building global development teams from the ground up. I spent about six months there, immersing myself in the local work culture and processes. One vivid memory that encapsulates the challenges of bureaucracy was the process of installing a simple software on my laptop. It was an ordeal that involved no less than five different people.

First, there was the individual responsible for actually installing the software, who had access to the installation files. Then, another person was needed to grant permissions to those files. A third person had to enter additional access credentials during the installation process. A fourth individual completed the setup, and finally, a fifth person was there to oversee the entire process to ensure all protocols were followed.

This experience was an eye-opener. While the intention behind such a multi-layered approach was to ensure security and compliance, it also highlighted a profound lack of trust in individual capabilities and autonomy. The process was slow, cumbersome, and, frankly, frustrating. It underscored how excessive control can stifle productivity and innovation.

Through this, I learned that trust plays a critical role in streamlining processes. By fostering a culture where individuals are trusted to handle tasks with greater autonomy, organizations can significantly reduce bureaucratic delays. For example, in our project, we started advocating for a more simplified process where trusted team members were given broader access rights to manage software installations independently. This change required a cultural shift towards valuing trust and accountability over rigid control.

It did not happen overnight, but the results were transformative. Not only did it speed up our development cycles, but it also empowered the team, instilling a sense of ownership and responsibility. By reducing unnecessary bureaucratic layers, we created a more agile and responsive environment, conducive to innovation and efficiency.

This experience in India underscored the importance of balancing necessary security protocols with a culture of trust. It showed that by empowering individuals and reducing red tape, organizations can unlock significant productivity gains and foster a more dynamic and innovative work environment.

What Can We Learn?

Expanding on the valuable lessons learned from the global practice of software engineering, especially considering the integration of remote work and the foundational trust required to operate effectively across diverse cultural landscapes.

The global software engineering field thrives on the cross-pollination of ideas. By incorporating successful strategies from one cultural context into another, companies can foster a dynamic and innovative working environment. For instance, the principle of 'Jugaad' from India, which emphasizes resourcefulness and flexibility, could be integrated into the structured environments typical of Western enterprises to enhance agility and problem-solving capabilities without sacrificing the rigor of systematic planning. This blend of adaptability with meticulousness can lead to enhanced innovation efficiency. We must adopt and adapt.

With the advent of remote work, geographical boundaries are becoming less significant, enabling unprecedented levels of collaboration. Remote work facilitates the fusion of diverse perspectives by connecting teams from different cultures and backgrounds without the need for physical relocation. This collaboration can lead to unique solutions that a homogeneous team might never consider. As we have already discussed, trust plays a crucial role in this setup; organizations that foster trust and provide robust digital communication tools (like Slack, Zoom, and Microsoft Teams) empower their teams to work effectively, regardless of physical location. Trust and flexibility in remote work setups not only boost morale but also enhance productivity and foster a culture of innovation.

In an era where software often serves a global user base, understanding and integrating cultural nuances into software design is crucial. This sensitivity can influence everything from UI/UX design to the functionality of the software, ensuring that it is accessible and efficient across different cultural settings. This approach not only broadens the market reach but also enhances user engagement and satisfaction.

As discussed in previous chapters, trust is a cornerstone of successful remote work and innovation. When teams trust that their cultural insights and unique perspectives are valued, they are more likely to contribute openly and creatively. Organizations that cultivate trust and demonstrate a commitment to ethical practices, including respect for privacy and transparent communication, are better positioned to harness the full potential of their diverse workforce.

These insights emphasize the importance of not just adopting innovative practices but also adapting them in culturally sensitive ways that respect and leverage global diversity. This approach not only enriches the software development process but also helps create products that are truly global in scope and appeal.

Conclusion: Embracing Cultural Diversity in Software Engineering

The landscape of software engineering is richly variegated, marked by a spectrum of cultural nuances that shape practices, expectations, and innovations across the globe. This diversity is not merely a hurdle to be navigated; it represents a profound opportunity, a reservoir of varied perspectives, techniques, and ideas that can significantly enhance the creativity and effectiveness of technological solutions.

Embracing cultural diversity within software engineering is essential for fostering an environment where innovation thrives. By integrating diverse cultural insights and practices, we can produce solutions that are not only technically sound but also broadly accessible and responsive to a variety of global needs and contexts. This approach does more than just expand market reach; it enriches the design and functionality of products, ensuring they are more inclusive and sensitive to the global user base.

Leveraging cultural diversity effectively means going beyond mere acknowledgment; it requires active integration and adaptation of varied practices. It calls for a collaborative, open-minded approach that values and utilizes the unique contributions of all team members, regardless of their cultural background. This can lead to breakthrough innovations that might not be possible within a monocultural team. As they say, "A single beam cannot support a great house." We need everyone's strength to build something truly magnificent.

Furthermore, the movement towards embracing cultural diversity must also consider remote work and trust dynamics, as discussed in previous chapters. Remote work enables teams to collaborate across borders without the need for physical relocation, while trust underpins the willingness to share and innovate freely. Together, these elements can dramatically enhance the potential for cross-cultural collaboration and innovation.

As we continue to advance in the technology sector, let us commit to these principles: valuing diverse perspectives, fostering an inclusive environment, and utilizing the full spectrum of global insights. This commitment not only fuels innovation but also ensures that our technological advancements contribute positively to society at large.

By championing cultural diversity, we not only enhance our capabilities in software engineering but also build towards a more inclusive and innovative future. This endeavor is not just beneficial; it is imperative for the continued growth and relevance of our industry in a rapidly globalizing world. Remember, "Diversity is the art of thinking independently together."

Chapter 15

Envisioning the Future of Software Engineering

TRENDS, TECHNOLOGIES, AND ROLES

Having navigated the diverse and intricate tapestry of global software engineering practices, we now turn our gaze forward to envision the future. It's like finishing a hearty global meal and now eyeing the dessert menu; what delights and challenges lie ahead?

As we navigate the swift currents of technological evolution, the field of software engineering stands on the brink of profound transformations. The relentless pace of innovation not only reshapes the tools and platforms we use but also redefines the very essence of the roles and skills required by today's engineers. This dynamic environment presents a spectrum of both formidable challenges and unprecedented opportunities.

This chapter delves deep into the emerging trends, cutting-edge technologies, and evolving roles that are sculpting the future landscape of software engineering. We will explore how the traditional paradigms are being disrupted and what it means for those who will navigate this new era. The digital landscape is being continuously redefined by several powerful forces such as technological advancements, globalization of technology, shifts in consumer expectations, and regulatory and ethical considerations.

Breakthroughs in fields such as artificial intelligence, machine learning, quantum computing, and the Internet of Things (IoT) are not only creating new opportunities but are also setting new standards of performance and efficiency. As software engineering becomes increasingly globalized, it necessitates a broader understanding and integration of diverse cultural and operational practices, which in turn influences software development methodologies and team dynamics.

Today's users demand faster, more personalized, and highly secure digital experiences, driving engineers to adopt more agile, user-centric approaches in software development. As the impact of software extends deeper into personal and public realms, software engineers increasingly find themselves at the crossroads of ethical dilemmas and regulatory requirements, which dictate a substantial portion of the development lifecycle.

This chapter will provide a roadmap for navigating these changes, identifying the skills and strategies that will enable software engineers to thrive. We will examine how emerging technologies are redefining problem-solving and innovation, discuss the integration of new security paradigms, and highlight the importance of continuous learning in staying relevant. Furthermore, we will explore how the fusion of technical prowess with enhanced soft skills is becoming critical in a multidisciplinary, interconnected world.

The goal is to arm current and future software engineers with the knowledge and insights needed to excel in this evolving environment. By the end of this chapter, you should have a clearer vision of how to adapt to and shape the future of software engineering, ensuring that you are not only a participant in this wave of change but also a driving force behind it.

Future Trends and Emerging Technologies in Software Engineering

Software engineering is rapidly evolving, driven by breakthroughs and integrations that are setting new paradigms for development and execution. Let's explore some key trends defining the future of our field.

Artificial Intelligence and Machine Learning (AI/ML)

AI and ML are not just buzzwords; they're revolutionizing software development, moving us from traditional coding to more sophisticated, data-driven approaches. AI's ability to automate complex decision-making processes is transforming everything from software testing to user interface design. Imagine having an AI that predicts user behavior, automates tedious tasks, and optimizes performance without any human intervention. It's like having a personal assistant who never sleeps or asks for a raise! We'll delve deeper into AI and ML in the next chapter, examining how engineers can harness these powerful tools to lead innovations in their fields, as this topic is very important and is redefining the roles.

Quantum Computing

Quantum computing, though still in its early stages, promises to overhaul how we solve the most complex problems that classical computers struggle with. Picture a computer solving problems so complex they make your toughest debugging sessions look like child's play. Quantum computing's potential impact on fields such as cryptography, material science, and complex system simulations is immense.

For software engineers, quantum computing offers a frontier of challenges and opportunities, requiring new thinking around algorithm design and data processing. As we venture into this frontier, the role of software engineers will evolve, necessitating the development of new skills and roles. So what is Quantum Computing?

Quantum computing uses principles of quantum mechanics to process information in ways classical computers cannot. This allows for efficient problem-solving in areas like cryptography, optimization, financial modeling, and drug discovery, where complexity overwhelms traditional methods. If software engineers want to evolve and stay current they must adopt some of the new skills that are needed for quantum computing.

Skills Needed for Quantum Computing

1. **Quantum Algorithm Design:** Engineers will need to understand quantum mechanics principles to develop algorithms that leverage quantum states like superposition and entanglement.
2. **Quantum Software Development:** With platforms like Qiskit by IBM and Microsoft's Quantum Development Kit, engineers will need to learn how to implement quantum algorithms within a software environment.
3. **Hybrid Systems:** Learning to integrate quantum computing solutions with classical systems will be crucial, as most real-world applications will operate on hybrid platforms that combine both technologies.

Quantum computing will reshape software engineering, giving rise to specialized roles like Quantum Algorithm Developers, Quantum Software Testers, and Quantum Integration Specialists. These roles will bridge the gap between quantum and classical computing, ensuring seamless operation across diverse platforms.

Quantum computing will profoundly affect various industries. In cryptography, for instance, quantum algorithms like Shor's algorithm pose a significant threat to traditional cryptographic securities, prompting the development of quantum-resistant cryptographic methods. Material science stands on the cusp of a revolution as quantum simulations promise the ability to discover new materials and drugs by simulating molecular structures and interactions with unprecedented accuracy. Additionally, quantum computing offers transformative potentials in optimization processes used across logistics, manufacturing, and service industries. And we must prepare for the Quantum future.

Preparing for the quantum future requires a strategic and proactive approach from both software engineers and organizational leaders. Continuous learning will be key, with an emphasis on courses, workshops, and certifications that keep professionals at the forefront of quantum advancements. Collaboration with physicists and quantum scientists will bridge the gap between abstract quantum mechanics and practical software applications.

Organizations must invest in the right resources, facilitate cross-disciplinary teams, and create a culture that encourages experimentation and supports quantum readiness. By prioritizing these strategies, software engineers and leaders can ensure they are well-prepared for the transformative impact of quantum computing and embrace the future.

As we look ahead, it's clear that the future of software engineering is both challenging and exhilarating. The integration of

AI, ML, and quantum computing represents a significant shift in the computational landscape, offering exciting opportunities to redefine the boundaries of what software can achieve. So, let's embrace these changes, stay curious, and keep learning, but that's not all. Other trends are emerging that will define the future of software engineering.

Internet of Things (IoT)

Another trend that will define the future of software engineering is the expanding **Internet of Things (IoT)** ecosystem, which is pushing software engineers to address unique challenges related to scalability, security, and user experience across billions of connected devices. Picture your refrigerator, toaster, and even your yoga mat sending data back and forth like old friends catching up. As everyday objects become data points, we must develop solutions that can handle vast amounts of data in real-time while ensuring these systems are secure against increasing threats.

The IoT is revolutionizing software engineering, transforming industries, and necessitating new roles that cater to an increasingly interconnected world. As sensors get embedded in everyday objects, the IoT merges the physical and online worlds, opening up a myriad of possibilities and challenges. It's like living in a sci-fi movie, but with slightly more troubleshooting.

In this brave new world, specialized roles are cropping up. For instance, the IoT Architect is crucial for designing the infrastructure that supports seamless communication between devices. They ensure scalability, reliability, and security within vast networks that connect everything from kitchen appliances to industrial machinery. Think of them as the air traffic controllers of the IoT, ensuring everything runs smoothly without any mid-air collisions.

The industries most transformed by IoT include manufacturing, healthcare, smart homes, and urban development. In manufacturing for example, IoT devices streamline operations through predictive maintenance and real-time monitoring, significantly enhancing efficiency and safety. If we look at the healthcare industry, we can see that IoT innovations lead to better patient monitoring systems and more personalized treatments. Smart homes integrate IoT to enhance comfort and energy efficiency, while smart city initiatives use IoT to optimize everything from traffic management to environmental monitoring.

Even the property and casualty (P&C) insurance sector is getting a makeover with IoT. The IoT promises transformative changes, particularly in how insurers assess risk, price policies, and manage claims. IoT devices enable insurers to gather real-time data directly from the insured entities, be it homes, vehicles, or commercial properties. For example, smart home devices can monitor everything from water leaks to electrical systems, and smart car technology can track driving behavior. This data allows insurers to assess risks more accurately and personalize insurance premiums based on actual usage and risk levels rather than relying on broader demographic data and statistical models. This usage-based insurance (UBI) is particularly prominent in auto insurance, where telematics devices collect data on driving patterns, distances driven, and adherence to traffic rules, allowing insurers to tailor premiums more closely to the individual risk each driver presents. It's like having a personal insurance assistant who knows everything about you, without the creepy factor, we hope.

IoT technology empowers insurers to move from a reactive to a proactive risk management approach. By analyzing data from IoT devices, insurers can identify potential risks before they result in claims. For instance, sensors in buildings can detect issues like pipe leaks or structural weaknesses, prompting early interventions that can prevent more significant damages and insurance claims. This not only saves costs but also enhances customer satisfaction by mitigating potential disruptions.

IoT also streamlines the claims management process, making it faster and more efficient. In the event of an accident or damage, IoT devices can automatically notify insurers and provide detailed data about the incident. For example, in the case of a car accident, IoT devices can send real-time data about the crash, such as the impact force and the conditions leading to the accident, which can help insurers quickly assess the claim without the need for extensive investigations. This speeds up the claims handling process, reduces the likelihood of fraud, and improves customer experiences during stressful times.

IoT allows insurers to engage with their customers in more meaningful ways, providing regular updates and advice on how to reduce risks. Insurers can offer value-added services such as maintenance alerts and safety recommendations based on the data collected from IoT devices. This ongoing engagement helps build stronger customer relationships and loyalty, as insurers are seen as partners in risk management rather than just financial safeguards.

The insights gained from IoT data can lead insurers to develop new products and services that meet the evolving needs of their customers. For example, new insurance products might include cyber insurance policies for smart homes or coverage extensions for autonomous features in vehicles.

The integration of IoT technology in P&C insurance not only transforms traditional practices but also creates opportunities for both insurers and insureds to benefit from more accurate risk assessments, enhanced loss prevention, efficient claims processing, and personalized customer interactions. As IoT continues to evolve, it will likely become an integral component of the insurance landscape, continuously driving innovation and improvement in the industry.

Preparing for the IoT-driven future requires a multi-faceted approach. Software engineers need to bolster their skills in network security, data analytics, and system integration. Understanding the specifics of IoT technology, such as sensor dynamics and the communication protocols that enable device connectivity, is essential. Furthermore, as the data generated by IoT devices is vast and varied, engineers must also develop competencies in managing and analyzing big data to derive actionable insights.

Organizations must invest in training and development programs to equip their engineers with these skills. Adopting a culture of continuous learning and adaptability is vital, as the IoT landscape is rapidly evolving. Companies must also prioritize security from the outset, embedding robust security measures into every layer of IoT infrastructure to protect against the increasing risks associated with device interconnectivity.

By proactively adapting to these changes, software engineers can lead the charge in harnessing the full potential of IoT, driving innovation across industries, and shaping a connected future that leverages technology to solve complex problems and improve quality of life.

But let's not sugarcoat it; IoT brings its own set of challenges. The vast amount of data generated needs to be securely managed and analyzed to provide actionable insights. And here's where we come in, software engineers, bolstering our skills in network security, data analytics, and system integration. It's a bit like being a digital janitor, but one who's also a data wizard.

DevSecOps

Another key trend is the rise of **DevSecOps**, integrating security practices throughout the development lifecycle. This isn't just about adding a final security check but embedding security into every phase of software creation and deployment.

Imagine building a house and checking for termites at every stage, from laying the foundation to putting up the wallpaper.

It is obvious that DevSecOps represents a cultural shift in software development. This approach ensures that security isn't just a final checkpoint but a foundational component of all phases of software creation and deployment. By considering security early in the development process, software engineers can address vulnerabilities early, mitigate risks more effectively and deliver safer, more resilient products.

Security is waved deeply into every stage of the development lifecycle. This integration of security is not merely an additional step but becomes a cornerstone, influencing everything from initial design to deployment and maintenance. The traditional model of bolting on security features towards the end of software development is no longer viable in today's fast-paced, security-conscious environment.

The benefits of adopting a DevSecOps approach are manifold. Early vulnerability detection reduces severe flaws later on, streamlining development and encouraging a culture of shared responsibility. Security becomes a common thread in the dialogue between developers, operations staff, and security professionals, fostering better communication and collaboration. It's like being in an orchestra where everyone knows their part and plays in perfect harmony. This proactive stance not only enhances the security posture of the final product but also streamlines the development process by reducing the need for disruptive mitigations after major issues are discovered during late-stage testing.

Moreover, integrating security throughout the development process encourages a culture of shared responsibility among all team members. Security becomes a common thread in the dialogue between developers, operations staff, and security professionals, fostering better communication and collaboration. This unity is crucial for the rapid development cycles characteristic of modern software projects, particularly in an agile framework.

To prepare for a future where DevSecOps is the standard, organizations and individual software engineers should start by enhancing their understanding of security principles. Education and training in contemporary security practices should be prioritized, including understanding the nature of threats, learning about the latest defensive technologies, and exploring the legal implications of software security.

In practice, the implementation of DevSecOps involves integrating security tools directly into development and deployment pipelines. Automated security scanning and threat modeling should become routine, with these tools running alongside the ones used for development and operations to provide real-time feedback. This immediate feedback allows teams to address issues promptly, drastically reducing the cycle time for security reviews and patches.

Furthermore, to truly embed security into the cultural fabric of development teams, organizations need to incentivize and reward security-oriented thinking. By making security a key performance indicator for all technical roles, companies can ensure that it is given the attention it deserves.

As the landscape of software development continues to evolve, embracing DevSecOps not only prepares organizations to handle emerging security threats more effectively but also positions them to lead in the creation of truly robust and reliable software solutions.

To prepare for this future, organizations must invest in training and development programs to equip engineers with the necessary skills. Adopting a culture of continuous learning and adaptability is vital, as the IoT landscape is rapidly evolving. Companies must also prioritize security from the outset, embedding robust security measures into every layer of IoT infrastructure to protect against the increasing risks associated with device interconnectivity.

By proactively adapting to these changes, software engineers can lead the charge in harnessing the full potential of IoT, driving innovation across industries, and shaping a connected future that leverages technology to solve complex problems and improve quality of life. It's a thrilling ride, and we're all strapped in together, ready to navigate the twists and turns of this technological rollercoaster.

In the next chapter, we'll delve deeper into how AI and ML are integrated into modern software practices. But for now, let's keep our eyes on the horizon and our minds open to the endless possibilities ahead. As the proverb goes, "A journey of a thousand miles begins with a single step", and we're just getting started.

A Story of Evolution: From Inspiration to Innovation

In the fast-paced world of technology, if you're not learning and evolving, you'll be left behind faster than you can say "JavaScript." Let me share a story that brings this point home..

About a little over a decade ago, I had a few colleagues who were my guiding stars. These were the folks who seemed to know everything about technology, integration, and the intricate technical parts of our projects. They were the ones I ran to whenever I hit a snag, and their desks were like the Oracle of Delphi for engineers like me. I would watch them in awe, wondering how they became so proficient and what secret rituals they performed to attain such knowledge. After all I had over a decade of software engineering experience myself, but these guys were really great.

Fast forward a few years, and the tables have turned in the most unexpected way. Today, I find myself as the innovator, the creator, and the source of inspiration for the next generation of engineers. Those same colleagues I once idolized are now somewhat in the dark, struggling to grasp the new technologies and cloud computing paradigms that are reshaping our field. It's a bit like watching the former high school star athlete who never adapted to the changing game. They are still good, but no longer great.

The harsh reality is that they didn't evolve. They rested on their laurels, confident in their established expertise, and believed they had reached the pinnacle of their careers. "We're senior engineers and architects now," they thought. "We've made it." But in the relentless march of technology, standing still is the same as moving backwards.

It's sad to witness, really. The once-great mentors are now merely good engineers, dutifully following orders and slowly being overshadowed by automation. They remind me of a sailboat that refuses to adjust its sails to the changing wind, drifting aimlessly while others navigate swiftly ahead. They thought they knew it all, but the truth is, in our field, knowing it all is a perpetual journey, not a destination.

For those of us who want to remain great and in demand, the lesson is clear: you must evolve and learn new trends continuously. Don't let your sailboat be pushed back by the wind of change. You must direct it forward with every new technology and development that comes your way.

Stay curious, stay hungry, and never stop learning. The tech world doesn't wait for anyone. Those who adapt and grow with the industry will always be the innovators and leaders, while those who don't might just find themselves looking back wistfully, wondering where they went wrong.

So, let's make a pact to always be on the lookout for new knowledge and to embrace change with open arms. After all, "The only constant in life is change," and it's those who master the art of adaptation that will continue to inspire and lead the way in the ever-evolving landscape of software engineering.

The Software Engineer of the Future

The role of software engineers is evolving faster than ever, stretching beyond the traditional boundaries and demanding a fusion of deep technical knowledge and sophisticated soft skills. As we look ahead, it's clear that the demands on software engineers will continue to grow, transforming them into hybrid professionals who not only write code but also navigate complex human interactions and strategic challenges. Software engineers are technically versatile, problem solvers and innovators, and of course lifelong learners.

Gone are the days when knowing one or two programming languages was enough. The software engineer of the future will need to master a diverse set of tools and technologies. With AI taking over routine coding tasks, the real value will lie in an engineer's ability to integrate these technologies to create innovative solutions. Whether it's cloud computing, blockchain, or quantum computing, engineers will need to be comfortable working with a vast array of technologies. Think of it as being a Swiss Army knife of tech, always ready with the right tool for the job.

Innovation will be at a premium. Future engineers will be valued for their ability to think creatively and solve complex problems. This isn't just about coding; it's about viewing challenges through a multidisciplinary lens, incorporating insights from data science, user experience design, and even ethical considerations. Imagine being part of a think tank where your role is not just to find the solution but to invent it from scratch.

To keep pace with rapid technological advancements, software engineers will need to commit to lifelong learning. This means continuously updating their knowledge with new programming languages, emerging software frameworks, and evolving best practices in areas like security and privacy. It's like being in a never-ending school, but one where the lessons are always fresh and exciting.

As projects increasingly involve collaboration across time zones and cultures, soft skills will become as critical as technical abilities. Effective communication, empathy, and teamwork will be essential. Future engineers will need to negotiate, resolve conflicts, and inspire team members, making them as much leaders as they are coders. Picture yourself as the captain of a ship, steering your team through the stormy seas of software development with both technical skill and a motivational pep talk.

In essence, the software engineer of the future will be a hybrid figure, which is equally versed in the intricacies of technology and the nuances of human collaboration. They'll be expected to not only develop code but also drive conversations around its deployment, ensuring solutions are innovative, ethically sound, and globally conscious. The ongoing evolution in this role will demand a dynamic blend of skills, pushing engineers to continuously adapt and refine their capabilities.

New Roles and Responsibilities

As technology forges new frontiers, the software engineering landscape is set to expand into diverse and specialized roles that reflect the need for innovation, ethical consideration, and deep technical expertise. Let's dive into some of the roles that will become central in the near future

- **AI Ethics Officer:** With AI everywhere, someone needs to ensure these technologies are implemented responsibly. Enter the AI Ethics Officer, who will oversee the ethical dimensions of AI deployments, from data privacy to avoiding biases. They'll be the moral compass guiding AI decisions, making sure we don't end up in a dystopian sci-fi scenario.
- **Quantum Algorithm Developer:** As quantum computing moves from theory to practice, the demand for Quantum Algorithm Developers will surge. These specialists will design algorithms for quantum machines, solving problems beyond the reach of classical computers. They'll revolutionize sectors like cryptography, optimization, and molecular modeling, potentially revolutionizing sectors like pharmaceuticals, finance, and cybersecurity. Think of them as the wizards of the digital realm, conjuring solutions out of quantum magic.
- **IoT Architect:** With IoT connecting everything from our fridges to our cities, IoT Architects will be crucial. They'll design and manage networks of interconnected devices, ensuring effective communication, efficiency, and security. Imagine being the mastermind behind a smart city,

where every device works in harmony to create a seamless living experience.

As the digital landscape is constantly evolving, bringing new challenges and opportunities, so too will the roles within software engineering, pushing professionals to adapt to these new challenges and opportunities. These emerging roles, such as AI Ethics Officers, Quantum Algorithm Developers, and IoT Architects, highlight the industry's shift towards more specialized, ethical, and technically complex disciplines. By anticipating these changes, current and future software engineers can prepare to not just participate in but drive the next wave of technological innovation, ensuring they remain at the forefront of their field. This diversification of roles will not only enrich the profession but also amplify its impact on society, emphasizing the critical interdependence of ethical standards, technical expertise, and innovative thinking in shaping the future.

These future roles will require a hybrid set of skills; technical depth, strategic insight, and ethical consideration, highlighting the complex interplay between rapid technological advancement and its broader societal impacts. As these roles develop, they will shape not only the future of software engineering but also the trajectory of how technology influences our world. This diversification will enrich the profession and amplify its impact on society, underscoring the critical interdependence of ethical standards, technical expertise, and innovative thinking in shaping the future. Let's embrace these changes, stay curious, and keep learning. After all, in the world of software engineering, the only constant is change.

How To Stay In Demand

In today's rapidly evolving technological landscape, software engineers must actively pursue opportunities and strategies to remain relevant and in demand. This isn't just about keeping up; it's about staying ahead, being the one who defines the trends rather than just following them. So, let's roll up our sleeves, put on our thinking caps, and dive into how we can stay in demand in this dynamic field.

To stay competitive, we need to stay abreast of emerging trends and technologies. Think of it as being a tech connoisseur, always on the lookout for the latest and greatest. Engaging with new developments through specialized training courses, hands-on projects, or contributing to open-source platforms can provide practical experience and a significant competitive edge. Remember, technology waits for no one. It's like a treadmill; if you stand still, you're going backwards.

The ability to adapt to changing technologies and market demands is more crucial than ever. We must adopt an agile mindset, not just in managing projects but also in our approach to career development and continuous learning. This agility enables us to quickly pivot our skills and methods to align with new industry standards and practices. Think of it as being a chameleon in the tech jungle, always blending with the latest trends to survive and thrive.

Beyond technical expertise, understanding the broader business context of projects is vital. We should strive to see beyond the code to the larger business impacts of our work. Aligning technical solutions with business objectives not only enhances the strategic value of our role but also ensures that our contributions are recognized and valued within our organizations. In other words, we need to be more than just code warriors; we need to be strategic ninjas.

The Demand for Cloud Computing and AI Skills

The demand for skilled software engineers is projected to continue growing, particularly in areas like AI, cybersecurity, and cloud computing. As automation and digital transformation initiatives become standard across industries, the need for professionals who can design, maintain, and improve these complex systems will remain high.

The demand for software engineers in cloud computing and AI is indeed robust and shows signs of continued growth. Of course each of these fields presents unique challenges and opportunities for software engineers, influencing not only their job security but also how they approach their roles and the sharing of knowledge.

Cloud computing has fundamentally transformed the infrastructure of nearly every tech-driven enterprise by offering scalable, flexible, and cost-efficient solutions. The increasing migration of services to the cloud by companies seeking to enhance their operational efficiencies ensures that the demand for skilled cloud engineers remains high. These professionals are needed to develop, manage, and secure cloud environments that support everything from data storage and virtual workspaces to AI-driven analytics and integrated IoT solutions.

As businesses increasingly rely on cloud platforms like AWS, Azure, and Google Cloud, the expertise required to navigate these environments, optimize resource use, and ensure data security is more crucial than ever. Software engineers with skills in designing cloud architecture, implementing cloud security measures, and managing large-scale cloud deployments are finding themselves in high demand. Think of it as being a cloud shepherd, guiding the flock of data safely through the skies.

In the realm of artificial intelligence, the scenario is a bit more nuanced. AI and machine learning rely heavily on data to train algorithms that can perform tasks ranging from simple automation to complex decision-making processes. This dependency on data could create a cautious environment where engineers might feel incentivized to withhold personal insights or innovative techniques to maintain their competitive edge.

However, the nature of AI development work often requires extensive collaboration and data sharing to create effective models. While some engineers might consider withholding knowledge as a way to safeguard their value to a company, this approach can stifle innovation and hinder the development of more sophisticated AI solutions. In practice, companies often encourage open collaboration and knowledge sharing to drive innovation. This is facilitated by implementing intellectual property protections and defining clear contributions in collaborative projects to ensure that individuals' contributions are recognized and rewarded. So how do we prepare to continue to be relevant?

Preparing for Continued Relevance

Well, software engineers can prepare for continued relevance in these high-demand areas by focusing on several key strategies.

1. Specialized Skills Development: For cloud computing, focus on gaining certifications and experience in leading cloud services, understanding architecture patterns, and mastering security best practices. For AI, delve into areas like neural networks, natural language processing, and reinforcement learning.

2. **Collaboration and Contribution:** Engage with the community through contributions to open-source projects and participation in collaborative research. This can help in building a professional reputation and staying connected with the latest developments.
3. **Ethical Considerations:** With AI, particularly, understanding the ethical implications of technologies and advocating for responsible AI practices will be crucial. This includes ensuring transparency, fairness, and privacy in AI systems.
4. **Continuous Learning:** Both fields are rapidly evolving, making continuous learning a necessity. This can be through formal education, online courses, workshops, or self-study.

In conclusion, while the temptation to withhold knowledge might exist in areas like AI, the broader benefits of collaboration and the necessity for continuous innovation in fields like cloud computing and AI generally promote an environment of shared learning and mutual advancement. This not only enhances individual careers but also drives the technological and ethical development of the industries involved.

By integrating these strategies, software engineers can ensure they not only remain relevant but also thrive in a future where technology and business needs are perpetually shifting. This proactive approach to career development will enable us to seize opportunities and meet the challenges of the future head-on, maintaining their status as indispensable assets in any tech-driven organization. After all, in the ever-changing world of technology, it's not just about keeping up; it's about leading the charge and making a lasting impact. Remember to be creative and innovate. So, let's stay curious, keep learning, and continue to innovate. Because, as they say, and we have also said it before in this book, but it is worth repeating, "The best way to predict the future is to create it."

Conclusion: Shaping the Future of Software Engineering

As we close this chapter on envisioning the future of software engineering, it's clear we are navigating an era marked by unprecedented technological evolution. From the rise of artificial intelligence and quantum computing to the pervasive spread of IoT and the integrative practices of DevSecOps, the landscape is rapidly changing. If we want to remain at the forefront of this transformation, we must cultivate a suite of versatile technical skills and embrace a continuous learning mindset. After all, the only constant in technology is change.

Adapting to these changes requires not just technical acumen but also a strong foundation in soft skills. The ability to collaborate effectively across global, culturally diverse teams, communicate clearly, and exhibit empathy will differentiate the successful engineers of the future. Imagine trying to solve a complex problem with a team spread across five time zones, each with their own unique perspective. Now, add in a dash of clear communication and a sprinkle of empathy, and you've got the recipe for a global innovation powerhouse.

Creativity remains a critical asset in our toolkit. As routine tasks become automated, our value will increasingly be measured by our ability to think outside the box, devise novel solutions to complex problems, and leverage technology to meet evolving needs. Let's face it, if a robot can do the monotonous tasks, our time is better spent on the fun stuff, like coming up with the next big thing.

Ultimately, staying relevant in our field means embracing an agile mindset, being prepared to pivot as new technologies and methodologies emerge, and understanding the broader business and social impact of our work. The engineers who will thrive are those who view changes not as hurdles but as opportunities to innovate and impact the world positively. As they say, "When life gives you lemons, make lemonade." Or in our case, when technology gives you a new challenge, make groundbreaking software.

By fostering a culture of continuous improvement, ethical consideration, and proactive adaptation, we can ensure we not only remain in demand but also contribute significantly to shaping the future of technology. This journey of transformation is not just about personal or professional growth but about advancing the entire industry in ways that benefit society as a whole. So, let's embrace the future with open minds, ready to learn, innovate, and lead the charge in this exciting field.

Chapter 16

Embracing AI in Software Development: A Call to Innovate, Not Stagnate

In the rapidly advancing technological era we inhabit, Artificial Intelligence (AI) has transcended the realm of buzzwords to become a fundamental force reshaping software development and problem-solving. Despite its transformative potential, a palpable hesitation lingers among some organizations, particularly those steered by leaders with limited technical insight. This reluctance can stifle innovation and may cause firms to lag in the fiercely competitive technological arena.

At the dawn of a new era in technology, AI stands as a pivotal force destined to reshape the landscape of software development. Far from being just a technological trend, AI is now an essential part of modern software engineering, embedded deeply within the processes that drive innovation and efficiency. As we delve deeper into the potential of AI, it's clear that this technology is not merely an option but a necessity for those looking to thrive in an increasingly competitive market.

However, embracing AI is often met with hesitation. This reluctance is especially prevalent among organizations led by decision-makers who may not fully grasp the technical nuances of AI. Such trepidation, rooted in a lack of understanding and clouded by common misconceptions, risks leaving these organizations a step behind in the relentless tech race. The fear that AI may replace human jobs or that it introduces insurmountable complexity into operations are but a few of the unfounded fears that hamper its integration.

AI's role in modern software development extends beyond mere automation of tasks; it is transforming the very essence of how problems are identified and solved. Through the automation of complex decision-making processes and the enhancement of user experiences, AI allows software engineers to focus on higher-level strategic problem-solving and innovation. Additionally, AI's capacity to process and analyze large datasets with unprecedented speed and accuracy is invaluable in a world where data-driven decision-making is paramount.

Much of the resistance to AI integration stems from misconceptions about AI's capabilities and its impact on the workforce. Concerns about job displacement and data security are significant, yet they often overshadow the potential benefits. These fears can be mitigated through education and transparent communication about AI's role as a tool that complements rather than replaces human intellect and creativity.

As pioneers at the frontier of technological innovation, our response to AI should not be of resistance but of proactive engagement. Embracing AI within software development practices is not just about keeping pace; it's about setting the pace for future innovations. By integrating AI, we ensure that our projects are not only more efficient and effective but also more aligned with the evolving needs of a rapidly changing world. We must look beyond the myths and embrace the substantial advantages AI brings to our field, ensuring that we are not merely participants in the digital transformation but active leaders shaping its trajectory.

This chapter invites software engineers and technology leaders alike to reevaluate their stance on AI, urging a shift from skepticism to strategic integration, thereby securing a competitive edge in the evolving digital landscape.

The Essential Role of AI in Modern Software Development

Artificial Intelligence (AI) and Machine Learning (ML) tools are instrumental in revolutionizing operations across various sectors. AI enhances efficiency and speed by automating routine programming tasks, swiftly analyzing extensive data sets, and detecting complex patterns that would elude human analysts. By delegating routine tasks to AI, software engineers can focus their expertise on strategic problem-solving and creative innovations. Moreover, AI's capability to identify and rectify errors in real-time boosts the quality and reliability of code, marking a significant leap in development practices.

Let's be real for a second. How many times have you found yourself buried under a mountain of repetitive coding tasks, wishing for a magic wand to wave it all away? Enter AI, your new coding sidekick. This isn't just about making our lives easier, though, let's be honest, that's a big part of it. AI tools are revolutionizing our workflow, and they're here to stay.

In the modern tapestry of software development, AI and ML have transcended their roles as mere facilitators of automation to become central pillars in enhancing the engineering process. These technologies are not just reshaping the workflow by automating everyday tasks but are also redefining the essence of software engineering by enabling developers to swiftly verify algorithms, optimize code efficiency, and enhance overall software quality.

AI tools are adept at analyzing large volumes of data and identifying complex patterns quickly; tasks that are time-consuming and often impractical for human analysts. This rapid analysis capability allows engineers to refine their algorithms continuously, ensuring that the software not only meets the functional requirements but also operates at peak efficiency. For example, instead of manually searching through resources or using trial and error to optimize a sorting algorithm, engineers can leverage AI to propose or even generate optimal code snippets based on the latest algorithms known for their efficiency and reliability. This not only speeds up the developmental process but also enhances the engineer's ability to innovate by freeing up valuable time.

Furthermore, AI's role in real-time error detection and correction is a game-changer. It acts as a rigorous, unfailing observer that ensures code quality is maintained from the earliest stages of development. By catching bugs and vulnerabilities early, AI tools significantly reduce the time and resources spent on debugging and testing, which traditionally are the most time-intensive parts of software development.

AI and ML are not just buzzwords thrown around at tech conferences to make presentations sound cooler. These tools are genuinely game-changers. Imagine having a tireless assistant who never sleeps, never takes a coffee break, and never complains about those late-night coding marathons. AI can sift through mountains of data faster than you can say "debugging nightmare," spotting patterns and anomalies that would take us hours, if not days, to find.

The integration of AI into software development tools, like IDEs that offer suggestions for code optimization or even automate entire chunks of code based on the developer's objectives, exemplifies how deeply AI is embedded in the process. These intelligent systems learn from each interaction, continuously improving their suggestions and corrections, which in turn enhances the developer's ability to produce cleaner, more efficient code.

By automating the boring, AI frees us up to do what we do best, and that is innovate. Remember that feeling when you finally cracked that complex problem? AI gives us more of those moments by taking over the grunt work. It's like having a junior developer who's brilliant at all the boring bits, leaving you to handle the fun, challenging stuff. And trust me, there's nothing more satisfying than knowing you can focus on designing that killer feature without getting bogged down by repetitive tasks.

And let's not forget AI's knack for real-time error detection. It's like having a super vigilant colleague who catches mistakes before you've even had your first cup of coffee. This means fewer bugs, less time spent on testing, and more reliable code. It's a win-win. No more pulling your hair out over missed semicolons or misplaced brackets. AI has got your back.

By embracing AI, software engineers are not just improving their workflow but are also positioned to be more creative and innovative. They can focus more on the unique aspects of their projects; designing better user experiences, conceptualizing innovative features, and tackling challenging problems that require deep, strategic thinking. This shift is not just about keeping pace with technological advancements but about leading the charge towards more sophisticated, intuitive, and impactful software solutions.

The Misconceptions Holding Adoption Back

Let's be honest, folks. We've all seen it. The hesitant look from a senior manager when you mention integrating AI into the project. It's as if you suggested replacing the coffee machine with a robot barista. While that sounds pretty cool to me, it's often met with a mix of fear and confusion. "What if it breaks? What if it takes our jobs? What if it decides to start a band and leaves us all behind?" Okay, maybe not the last one, but the concerns are real and often exaggerated.

The resistance to AI integration often stems from a blend of misconceptions and a fundamental misunderstanding of AI's capabilities and mechanisms. Think of it like a bad sci-fi movie. AI is portrayed as this omnipotent entity that's out to get us, and every robot in the corner of our office is just waiting for its moment to turn against humanity. But here's the kicker: AI is more like a friendly sidekick than a villain. Let's break down a few major areas of concern: security, the fear of job replacement, complexity, and plain old misunderstanding.

Security Concerns: The apprehension about the security of AI tools like ChatGPT is a primary obstacle. The concern is that these platforms, which process vast amounts of data, might expose sensitive information or be susceptible to misuse. But let's put this fear to bed. AI tools are designed with layers of security, specifically meant to protect the data they handle. Companies like OpenAI ensure that data processed through tools like ChatGPT are handled in accordance with strict privacy standards and are not used for any other purposes than what is intended by the user.

For instance, when you chat with ChatGPT, your data inputs are used only to generate relevant responses and not stored for any future use without explicit user consent. It's like having a digital bouncer who checks IDs and lets only the good stuff in. And now Apple and other companies are partnering with OpenAI and integrating it in the phones and other tools.

Security protocols in AI applications are robust, incorporating advanced encryption and authentication measures to ensure that data remains secure and that access is controlled rigorously. The real challenge lies not in the inherent security risks of using AI but in ensuring that these systems are integrated with existing security frameworks to enhance overall system integrity without stifling innovation.

Fear of Replacement: Another significant misconception is the fear that AI will replace human jobs, particularly in fields like software engineering. While AI can automate certain tasks, such as code compilation, bug fixes, or even some levels of coding itself, it is not a substitute for human creativity, problem-solving capabilities, and critical thinking. For example, while an AI might generate a basic sorting algorithm based on predefined parameters, it lacks the capability to understand the unique context or deeper business needs that a human developer can comprehend and incorporate into more complex project elements.

Instead of viewing AI as a replacement, we should see it as a tool that complements and enhances our skills. AI can handle tedious, repetitive tasks, allowing us software engineers to focus on more strategic, creative aspects of software development such as designing the architecture of complex systems, creating innovative application features, or improving user experience; areas where human insight and creativity are irreplaceable.

Complexity and Misunderstanding: The perceived complexity of Artificial Intelligence is a significant barrier to its adoption, particularly among non-technical leaders who may view AI as an arcane and incomprehensible technology. This lack of understanding can foster mistrust and reluctance to integrate AI into business processes, despite its potential benefits.

AI systems, at their core, involve algorithms that are designed to mimic human intelligence processes through learning and decision-making. The inner workings of these algorithms, which involve data processing, pattern recognition, and machine learning, can indeed be complex and difficult for those without a technical background to understand. This complexity is not just in how AI functions but also in how it is developed, deployed, and maintained.

For instance, AI development involves various sophisticated elements like neural networks, natural language processing, and robotics, among others. Each of these components requires a deep understanding of both the underlying technology and the specific applications it serves. The complexity increases with the integration of AI into existing systems, requiring a careful balance between new AI capabilities and legacy infra-structure.

The intricacy of AI can lead to misunderstandings about its capabilities and limitations, which can lead to mistrust. Non-technical leaders might fear that AI could make unpredictable decisions, be difficult to control, or become too autonomous. There is also a concern about AI being a "black box," where decisions are made without transparent reasoning, making it hard for leaders to trust the outcomes fully.

Moreover, AI applications often require significant data input, and there can be concerns about the quality and integrity of this data. Misunderstandings about how AI uses data can lead to fears about privacy violations and ethical breaches, further compounding the trust issues.

How do we bridge the gap? To overcome these challenges, it's essential for organizations to invest in education and training for all stakeholders, especially non-technical leaders. Simplifying the complexities of AI through workshops, seminars, and hands-on demonstrations can demystify the technology and showcase its practical benefits.

Creating interdisciplinary teams that include both technical and non-technical members can facilitate better understanding and communication. These teams can serve as AI ambassadors within the organization, explaining AI projects in accessible language and demonstrating how AI decisions are made and monitored.

Enhancing transparency around how AI systems work and are governed can also alleviate fears. This means not just explaining the outcomes of AI processes but also detailing how decisions are reached. Establishing clear guidelines and ethical standards for AI use within the organization can help build trust. Implementing robust governance frameworks that include accountability for AI decisions ensures that AI systems align with organizational values and comply with regulatory requirements.

By addressing the complexities of AI head-on and striving for transparency and inclusiveness in AI initiatives, organizations can foster a culture of trust and curiosity around AI technologies, encouraging their thoughtful and effective integration into business processes.

There is a light at the end of the AI tunnel. Understanding and addressing these misconceptions is crucial for broader AI adoption. Educational initiatives that demonstrate how AI tools operate and how they enhance human work rather than replace it can help mitigate fears. Moreover, showcasing AI's role in augmenting security rather than compromising it can change the narrative around the risks associated with its use in the industry.

By demystifying AI and promoting its benefits, we can move towards a more informed, efficient, and innovative future in software development. It's about harnessing AI to create more value, not less, and to open new avenues for human creativity and technological advancement. So, let's roll up our sleeves, embrace the AI revolution, and show the world that we're not just keeping up with the times; we're setting the pace!

IntelliJ and Java: A Comparative Perspective

AI isn't here to steal your job or your favorite coffee mug. It's here to make our lives easier. Remember that time when debugging felt like searching for a needle in a haystack? Well, AI can help turn that haystack into a neat pile, with the needle gleaming on top. AI can automate the monotonous tasks, leaving us free to focus on what we do best; innovating, solving complex problems, and yes, maybe even having a bit more time for that extra cup of coffee.

Integrated Development Environments (IDEs) with AI capabilities are the epitome of this revolution. They offer smart suggestions, optimize your code, and even generate entire blocks of code based on what you're working on. These tools learn from every interaction, getting better and more accurate over time. It's like having an apprentice who gets smarter every day, only without the risk of them running off to start their own company.

Drawing a comparative perspective between well-established software tools like IntelliJ and emerging AI technologies helps elucidate the utility and necessity of embracing AI in software development. Much like IntelliJ, which has become indispensable for its capacity to enhance coding efficiency through features like code completion, debugging, and static code analysis, AI tools offer similar enhancements but on a broader scale.

Just as IntelliJ and similar tools revolutionized the way developers write, test, and debug code, AI technologies are poised to transform the landscape of software development even further. For instance, AI can automate more than just unexciting tasks; it can predict code errors before they occur, recommend optimizations, and even generate code snippets. This does not diminish the developer's role but rather augments their capabilities and frees them to focus on more complex and creative aspects of software development.

Comparing AI with tools like IntelliJ also helps demystify AI. Just as developers learned to integrate IntelliJ into their Java development environments, they can similarly learn to integrate AI tools into their development processes. This integration should be seen as an augmentation that complements the developers' skills, not as a replacement that threatens their roles.

Advocating for AI Integration

It's time we address the elephant in the room. No, AI isn't going to become sentient and start running the company (though that might make for an interesting movie plot). The key to overcoming these fears is education. We need to demystify AI, showing it as the powerful ally it is. Through workshops, training sessions, and a few well-placed jokes, we can help everyone from the intern to the CEO understand that AI is here to work with us, not against us. Here are three top things that we need to do:

1. **Educate and Demonstrate:** It's crucial to clearly illustrate how AI can seamlessly integrate into existing systems. This involves demonstrating AI's compatibility with current workflows and its potential to enhance the capabilities of the software engineering team, all while maintaining rigorous security standards.
2. **Promote a Culture of Innovation:** Encouraging a workplace environment that values experimentation and the adoption of cutting-edge technologies is essential. This cultural shift ensures that teams are not just keeping

pace with technological advancements but are also leveraging them to maintain a competitive edge.

3. **Develop AI Policies:** Establishing comprehensive guidelines that govern the safe and ethical application of AI tools in development projects is imperative. These policies should ensure that AI implementations align with both organizational values and industry standards, thereby fostering trust and transparency.

Imagine a world where you're not just keeping up with the Joneses but setting the pace. That's what embracing AI can do for us. By integrating AI into our projects, we're not just adopting new tools; we're becoming the trendsetters, the trailblazers in our field. And let's face it, who doesn't want to be known as the innovator in the room?

In conclusion, viewing AI as an advanced tool akin to IntelliJ or other development aids allows organizations to better appreciate and integrate these technologies into their workflows. By embracing AI, companies can enhance their productivity, foster innovation, and remain competitive in the rapidly evolving tech landscape.

So, let's embrace these changes, stay curious, and keep learning. Let's not be the ones left behind, staring at our outdated code while the rest of the world moves forward. As we dive into this chapter, let's remember that AI isn't just a tool; it's a game-changer. And in this game, we're here to win.

Conclusion: The Future Is Now

As pioneers and thought leaders in technology, we must champion the integration of AI into software development practices. Embracing AI not only augments our capabilities but also positions our organizations at the forefront of innovation and market relevance. Let us not fall behind due to misconceptions and unfounded fears; instead, let us lead by example, utilizing the most advanced tools available to propel our industries forward.

Engaging with AI in software development is not merely a technical upgrade; it is a strategic imperative that requires us to rethink and reshape our approaches to stay ahead. As we navigate through the accelerating currents of technological innovation, the integration of AI into software development is not just a trend; it's a pivotal shift that defines the future of our industry. AI's capacity to enhance, automate, and optimize is transforming how we approach design, problem-solving, and implementation, allowing us to tackle challenges with unprecedented speed and efficiency.

Embracing AI within software development catalyzes a transformation that extends beyond mere technological advancement; it signifies a commitment to staying at the cutting edge of innovation and securing a competitive edge in the market. AI tools like advanced machine learning algorithms and data analysis techniques are not just augmenting our capabilities; they are fundamentally redefining what it means to be a software engineer today.

For our organizations to thrive and lead in the dynamically evolving tech landscape, we must actively dismantle the misconceptions that hinder AI adoption. The fears of AI replacing human creativity are unfounded; instead, AI serves as a complement that enhances human ingenuity. By automating routine tasks, AI frees engineers to focus on complex problem-solving and strategic innovations, thereby elevating the creative aspects of software development.

As we move forward, it is essential that we foster a culture that not only accepts but also embraces AI as a core component of software engineering. This involves educating teams on AI's potential, integrating AI tools into existing workflows, and developing strategies to mitigate any risks associated with its use.

To truly realize AI's potential, we must not only adopt it ourselves but also advocate for its integration across our industry. This means creating policies that support safe and ethical AI use, offering training and resources to help teams understand and leverage AI technology, and fostering an environment where experimentation and innovation are encouraged.

As we conclude this discussion, I invite you to reflect on how AI is being integrated into your development processes. What challenges have you faced, and what strategies have you employed to overcome resistance to AI adoption? Your experiences and insights are invaluable as we collectively navigate this exciting era of software development.

Remember that by embracing AI, we are not just adapting to new technological standards; we are actively shaping the future of software engineering; a future where our creativity and innovation are amplified by the tools we employ. Let's continue to push the boundaries, innovate responsibly, and lead our teams towards a more efficient, effective, and exciting future in software development.

As the proverb goes, "He who is not courageous enough to take risks will accomplish nothing in life." Let's be courageous, embrace AI, and shape the future of software engineering together.

Chapter 17

Engineers as Chefs: Crafting Masterpieces in Software Development

In the world of software development, the distinction between merely coding and crafting truly impactful software is akin to the difference between someone who cooks and a chef who creates culinary masterpieces. It's often said that "everyone can code, but not everyone can be a software architect," much like the culinary world's adage, "everyone can cook, but not everyone can be a chef." These phrases underscore a fundamental truth about the nature of skill and creativity in highly technical and artistic fields. This chapter delves into the intricate parallels between software engineering and the culinary arts, demonstrating how exceptional engineers, akin to great chefs, blend creativity with profound technical skills to forge not just functional but extraordinary software creations.

The comparison extends beyond mere metaphor; it encapsulates the essence of what it means to be at the pinnacle of one's craft. Whether in a Michelin-starred kitchen or a Silicon Valley tech hub, the top professionals do more than follow recipes or algorithms; they innovate, redefine norms, and set new benchmarks for excellence. In this exploration, we'll uncover how the artistry of software engineering mirrors that of culinary mastery, where every line of code, like every ingredient, plays a pivotal role in creating something remarkable.

In software engineering, the convergence of technical skill and creative vision heralds a new era where engineers are not merely practitioners but artists. This artistic dimension is what elevates a proficient coder to the stature of a software architect, akin to how a chef transforms simple ingredients into a gastronomic experience. These exceptional engineers leverage their comprehensive understanding of technologies to create software that not only functions efficiently but also pushes the boundaries of what is possible, making each solution an innovative masterpiece.

Much like chefs who expertly blend ingredients to delight the senses, superior software engineers wield their deep understanding of technology to craft solutions that transcend ordinary expectations. These engineers possess a unique blend of qualities as I define them below:

- **Creative Vision:** Great software engineers see beyond the immediate task at hand. They have the foresight to predict emerging trends and user needs, crafting applications that are not only functional but also ahead of their time. This vision is similar to how a chef imagines a dish that can evoke a particular emotion or memory, aiming not just to satisfy hunger but to offer a memorable dining experience. Beyond meeting the basic requirements, they envision and develop software that is pioneering, intuitive, and exceeds the anticipated.

· **Technical Mastery:** Just as a chef masters the knife, a software engineer's prowess in coding is fundamental. Yet, the essence of their expertise extends into the orchestration of complex systems, the seamless integration of new technologies, and the architectural prowess that ensures software is not only robust but scalable. This deep technical mastery allows them to manipulate the basic building blocks of software development to create solutions that are elegant and effective.

· **Problem-Solving Flair:** Each project presents a unique set of challenges, reminiscent of the dietary restrictions or ingredient availability a chef might face. The best software engineers, like culinary masters, excel in adapting their approach to these challenges. They tweak algorithms, adjust architectures, and sometimes invent entirely new methods to address the needs at hand. Their approach is one of creative problem-solving, where the standard solutions do not suffice, and innovation becomes the key to success.

In essence, the artistry of software engineering lies in this blend of vision, mastery, and innovation. It's about seeing the code not just as lines of instructions but as a canvas for creative expression. It's about embracing the role of an artist who uses technology as their medium to build not just software but a legacy of innovation.

Not Just Coding; It is Creating

The philosophy of "Not Just Coding; It is Creating" in software development profoundly mirrors the artistic journey from cooking to culinary mastery. This concept transcends the mere assembly of code into a dynamic process of crafting innovative digital solutions, akin to how a chef transforms basic ingredients into a gastronomic feast.

Innovation versus Routine: In the realm of software engineering, routine coding is akin to following a recipe; functional but often lacking in flair. True creation in software development, however, is about reimagining the entire spectrum of possibilities. It involves pushing the boundaries of what can be done with technology, much like a chef experimenting with new techniques and ingredients to create a unique dish. This approach encourages engineers to explore uncharted territories, develop new technologies, and solve problems in revolutionary ways that fundamentally change how we interact with the digital world.

Custom Solutions: Just as a chef might alter recipes to cater to specific tastes or dietary needs, software engineers tailor applications to address the unique challenges and requirements of their users. This customization goes beyond mere functionality; it involves understanding the end-user's environment, preferences, and pain points to deliver a solution that fits seamlessly into their lives. This might mean developing user-friendly interfaces, optimizing software for better performance under specific conditions, or ensuring that the software integrates flawlessly with existing systems.

Aesthetic and Functional Harmony: The art of software development is not solely concerned with technical efficacy but also with the elegance and intuitiveness of the design. Similar to how a chef presents a dish that appeals to the senses, software engineers strive to create applications that are pleasing to use. This involves thoughtful interface design, logical navigation, and harmonious integration of elements, ensuring that the software is not only functional but also engaging. The goal is to enhance the user's experience by making the interaction with the software as enjoyable and intuitive as possible.

In embracing these principles, software engineers elevate their craft to an art form, where each line of code contributes to a larger vision. This vision seeks to blend functionality with creativity, leading to innovations that are not only technologically advanced but also impactful and meaningful in the everyday lives of users. By viewing ourselves as creators, we engineers can redefine the scope of our work and our contributions to the tech industry, pushing beyond traditional boundaries and fostering an environment where technology meets creativity.

The evolution from a coder to an architect in software engineering embodies a transition into a role that encompasses leadership, strategic vision, and mentorship, alongside technical expertise. This transformation is akin to a chef moving from cooking individual dishes to overseeing the entire kitchen, ensuring that everything runs smoothly, creatively, and efficiently.

Much like a chef plans a menu that can be consistently and efficiently prepared for a large number of guests, an engineer must design systems that can handle increased loads and demands without compromising performance. This involves understanding the intricacies of scalability and the ability to anticipate and solve potential issues before they arise. It requires a comprehensive approach to architecture that balances immediate functionality with future growth, ensuring that the systems can evolve and expand without significant overhauls.

In the same way that chefs mentor their kitchen teams, senior engineers play a crucial role in guiding and nurturing less experienced colleagues. This mentorship extends beyond technical guidance; it involves instilling a culture of excellence, creativity, and continuous improvement. Senior engineers must be role models, demonstrating not only how to code but how to approach problems strategically and innovatively.

This leadership helps build cohesive teams that are capable of tackling complex challenges collaboratively.

Engineers, like chefs, must look beyond the immediate task to consider the broader implications of their decisions. Strategic planning in software development involves understanding how technical choices impact the business, the end-users, and the long-term goals of the organization. Engineers must think like strategists, considering factors such as maintainability, scalability, user experience, and overall system integration. This holistic approach ensures that the software not only meets current requirements but is also positioned to adapt to future needs.

Engineers in leadership roles often face unique challenges that require innovative solutions. Like chefs adjusting recipes based on available ingredients or dietary restrictions, we engineers must adapt our problem-solving strategies to meet specific project constraints and requirements. This adaptability and creative problem-solving are what set great engineers apart, enabling them to devise solutions that are both effective and elegant.

A key aspect of being an architect is empowering the team to excel. This involves fostering an environment where team members feel valued and motivated to contribute their best work. By promoting open communication, encouraging experimentation, and providing the necessary resources and support, senior engineers can cultivate a productive and innovative team culture.

The role of an engineer as an architect requires a balance between deep technical knowledge and strategic vision. Engineers must stay abreast of the latest technological advancements while also understanding how these technologies can be leveraged to achieve business objectives. This dual focus enables them to make informed decisions that drive both technical excellence and strategic growth.

As software engineers ascend to the role of architect, they embrace a multifaceted responsibility that extends beyond coding. They become leaders, mentors, and strategic planners, guiding their teams and shaping the future of their projects. By balancing technical expertise with strategic insight, these engineers play a pivotal role in driving innovation and ensuring the success of their organizations. Just as chefs transform ingredients into culinary masterpieces, software engineers as architects transform ideas into groundbreaking technological solutions.

Conclusion: Embracing the Craft

Great software engineers are, at their core, much like masterful chefs; artists who bring a blend of passion, creativity, and meticulous skill to their craft. They contribute more than just technical expertise; they infuse their work with innovation and a commitment to excellence that elevates their creations to extraordinary levels.

As we forge ahead in our careers, let us aspire not merely to code but to create; to transform the raw ingredients of technology into solutions that innovate, inspire, and lead. This approach not only enriches our professional lives but also advances the field of software engineering, making it as dynamic and impactful as the world of haute cuisine.

By viewing software development through the lens of artistry, we can foster a culture of continuous improvement and innovation. We can build systems that are not only functional but also elegant, intuitive, and ahead of their time. Embracing the role of the engineer as an artist and architect will enable us to push the boundaries of what is possible, creating software that not only meets the needs of today but anticipates the demands of tomorrow.

In essence, being a great software engineer is about more than just writing code; it's about crafting solutions that resonate with users and stakeholders alike. It's about being a visionary who sees the potential in technology and brings it to life with creativity and precision. As we continue to evolve in our careers, let us strive to be the chefs of the software world, creating masterpieces that leave a lasting impact.

As we reach the end of this journey, reflecting on the numerous facets of software engineering discussed throughout this book, it becomes clear that creativity is not just a nice-to-have but a critical component for innovation. We have explored how interruptions and short meetings can break an engineer's workflow, how the distinction between good and great engineers often lies in their ability to embrace and adapt to new technologies like AI and cloud computing, and how middle management roles must evolve to stay relevant.

Much like chefs creating recipes through trial and error, engineers must be given the freedom to innovate, fail, and ultimately succeed. This process is essential for growth and excellence in any field. As engineers, we must strive to be more than just coders; we must be creators who blend technical mastery with a relentless pursuit of innovation.

As I conclude, I am reminded of a proverb: "A smooth sea never made a skilled sailor." Embrace the challenges, learn from failures, and continue to innovate. It is this mindset that will keep us at the forefront of technology, driving progress and creating software solutions that are not just functional but extraordinary.

Thank you for joining me on this exploration of the art and science of software engineering. Let's keep pushing the boundaries, one line of code at a time. And please remember, innovation isn't just about creating something new; it's about improving what exists and finding better ways to solve problems. So, stay curious, keep learning, and never be afraid to push the boundaries of what's possible. Your greatest work is yet to come.

Thomas Holmengren is a visionary force in the realms of software engineering and photography. With over 25 years of rich, diverse experience, he has carved out a distinguished career that spans continents and industries. Holding a master's degree in computer science, Thomas has excelled in various roles, from developer to global delivery manager, IT consultant, enterprise and solution architect, and now Senior Principal Software Engineer. His journey across Europe, Canada, the United States, India, and the Pacific has granted him unparalleled global insights, allowing him to integrate diverse technological practices and cultural perspectives into his work.

Thomas's expertise extends across telecommunications, financial services, government projects, and property and casualty insurance. His versatility and adaptability have honed his ability to deliver tailored solutions that drive growth and innovation. A results-driven and innovation-focused technology leader, Thomas consistently pushes the boundaries of what is possible in software development and integration frameworks. His groundbreaking work in cloud computing, artificial intelligence, and the latest technological advancements has set new industry standards.

Beyond the tech world, Thomas is also author and a passionate photographer with an insatiable drive to capture the wild wonders of our world. His photography celebrates the untamed beauty of nature, exploring the extraordinary tapestry of wildlife, landscapes, and cultures. His lens is a compass, guiding him to new adventures and experiences, and his work invites others to join him in this visual odyssey. His previous work includes *"Kenya Unveiled: A Safari Adventure"*.

Thomas's professional ethos centers around collaboration. He has worked closely with C-level executives, sales, marketing, and almost every department within organizations, gaining a holistic understanding of business operations and the critical role of technology in driving success. His career is a testament to his belief in innovation over stagnation, inspiring many in the field to pursue excellence.

Whether capturing the essence of wildlife or driving disruptive technological solutions, Thomas Holmengren's work is a celebration of creativity, technological mastery, and the relentless pursuit of progress. As a thought leader and true innovator, he continues to shape the future of software engineering, driving progress and excellence in ever-evolving landscapes. His legacy is one of groundbreaking contributions that enhance technological capabilities and inspire a deeper appreciation for the beauty and potential of our world.